A Personal

Jesus – Or

Not

Exploring Evidence For and Against the
Christian Worldview

Brace E. Barber

A Personal Decision for Jesus – Or Not; Exploring Evidence For and Against the Christian Worldview
ISBN 978-0-9678292-7-2 Copyright © 2020

See Companion Book; *TESTED: A New Strategy for Keeping Kids in the Faith* to learn the facts about the loss of kids from the faith and why the Christian church – or at least parents – must take action now.

Brace E. Barber
Thompson's Station, TN 37179
b@bracebarber.com

Other works by Brace E. Barber
- TESTED: A New Strategy for Keeping Kids in the Faith
- RANGER SCHOOL, No Excuse Leadership www.RangerSchool.com
- The Art of War Organized for Decision Making

Dedication

My wife and I dedicate this book to our children, Brace, Ethan and Sophia. They are the reason this mission to prepare kids to battle the world took on urgency several years ago. We pray that we have been good stewards of them as God's children. Each of them has provided invaluable insights to us. Through their feedback, they have challenged us to teach them more effectively. They have endured the years of teaching, testing and questioning that have accompanied our enthusiastic embrace of the evidence God has provided in support the reliability of His Word.

Acknowledgements

My wife, Natasha, is my biggest encourager. She is also my toughest sounding board. I have a tendency to fall in love with my *perfect* ideas. She has a way of lovingly letting me know that some of them are not so perfect. She has refined me and focused me more times that I can count and she has been my partner in forming this book. I am exceedingly grateful to God for her.

In any long-term endeavor like this there are countless people who have contributed and participated. Loren Ware provided the conversation that God used to convicted me of the importance of the task. Mark Campbell took time to provide expert guidance on what and how to attack the problem. Steve King and Mark Millard expended great amounts of imagination and energy in helping me with messaging and my introductory video. Hoyt Condra, Jason Carson, Paul Wilkinson and Wes Sellers provided some great perspective as did Todd and Cindy Parish, Johnny Dorris and John Leech. Ben and Alison Calhoun, Warwick and Tanya Burns and many others. Jason Ellerbrook and Maurice Painter have been enthusiastic about the project and about supporting it in the market.

A Personal Decision for Jesus – Or Not
Exploring Evidence For and Against the Christian Worldview

Contents

Preface

To the Parents and Pastors

Christian parents know that their children's decision to follow Jesus must be a personal one. It is a decision that must be wrestled with and settled in the mind and heart of each person. This study is the wrestling mat for that decision. However, unlike the most youth groups and the secular world, this Apologetics Bible Study provides a fair competition where the real scientific, historic and philosophical evidences are revealed. The truth is that the evidence overwhelmingly supports the Christian worldview, but that's not the point. The point is that your teens read, debate and decide for themselves.

To the Wrestlers

This entire study revolves around how seriously you will decide to take the Bible. My purpose is first to help you secure a reasonable belief in the Christian worldview and second, to get you to align your life to Scripture more closely. Though those are my goals, I try to frame the evidence for each of our subjects in a way that gives you the ability to consciously choose which path you are going to take. Make a personal decision for Jesus Christ, - or Don't. It is your choice, however, you should be aware of the implications of whichever choice you make.

I have presented the implications of your choices with each chapter. If you choose to remain or become a Christian, do not be deluded into thinking that is enough. God gave you his message in the form of the Bible. He sent his guidance to you for your daily living! He did it for a reason.

The Great Commission in Matthew 28:18-20 says,

"[18] Then Jesus came to them and said, 'All authority in heaven and on earth has been given to me. [19] Therefore go and make disciples of all nations, baptizing them in the name of the Father and of the Son and of the Holy Spirit, [20] and teaching them to obey everything I have commanded you. And surely I am with you always, to the very end of the age.'"

If you choose to leave the Christian Church, then do not be deluded into thinking that everything is the same except that you do not believe in Jesus Christ or God anymore. You have accepted a worldview that unashamedly admits that there is no ultimate meaning, value or purpose to life. Without the explanation of God as the cause and creator, the Universe and life happened by an extraordinary accident.

As an atheist/agnostic, you get to choose your own path and you get to change it any time you want. You are not able to logically say that one person is right while another is wrong. There is no standard for good or evil, only personal preferences. You have to accept that relativism (*there is no objective right or wrong*) rules your judgements on good and evil. The Nazi's preferred to kill Jews, the early leaders of the United States preferred to legalize slavery, and Muslims around the world prefer to mutilate the genitalia of young girls. You may not prefer it, but you cannot say that those cultures were wrong.

Welcome to the choice.

Introduction

Honor

The heels of my shoes tapped-tapped-tapped as walked down the barracks hallway passing the light brown doors of rooms on either side. As I passed one of the rooms the laughter coming from behind the door upset me. I was angry that they were still at West Point and hoped the honor board investigating their behavior would make a decision soon and kick them out. The two cadets in the room were guilty of a clear honor violation and they needed to go.

The West Point Honor Code is more than words. It is a standard of conduct that demands unequivocal integrity and it inflicts dire consequences in cases of dishonesty. The code reads, "A Cadet will not lie, cheat, steal or tolerate those who do."

> ## A CADET WILL NOT LIE, CHEAT, STEAL OR TOLERATE THOSE WHO DO

Cadets who violate that code are kicked out of the school. Within weeks the two cadets in the room I passed were removed from the ranks of the school. West Point does not try to rehabilitate liars, cheats and thieves; they remove them from the ranks for good because if they were allowed to graduate and have the opportunity to lead soldiers in battle their flawed judgement would potentially cost people their lives.

Now you might think that the harshest consequences were reserved for the biggest offenses, but you'd be wrong. Stealing items from people was treated the same as indicating you were in one place when you were actually in another. That black-and-white standard is extreme by today's measure, but all cadets know the rules and agreed to live by them.

Integrity is the highest principle of leadership where lives are on the line. As we deal with the truth or fallacy of Christianity, it is a black-and-white decision and your life is on the line. Your peace is on the line. West Point knows that when a person acts with integrity they are at peace with themselves. West Point produces leaders that are confident and sure on the battlefield. A person of integrity acts in ways that do not violate their beliefs. They do not cause internal conflict by acting hypocritically.

Unfortunately, a great number of Christians struggle to have this type of internal integrity. Many Christians are not at peace within themselves because of the conflict between their intellect and their faith. Their intellect tells them that scientific evidence points away from the existence of God while their faith says that God loves them. This struggle produces people who are meek and unsure. This self-perceived hypocrisy keeps them from spreading the gospel. These Christians carry around a sense of dishonesty that they do not know how to shake.

What if you got into a conversation about the reliability of the Bible with a person in the locker room at your gym? They casually say, "Oh. I stopped believing in that fairy tale when I graduated high school. Don't tell me you still buy into it."

What if while riding with a friend from school when they say, "I could never worship a God that would allow such evil in the world."

Are you confident in engaging in a conversation that presents the evidence and logic behind why the Bible is reliable and how evil exists in a world created by a loving God? The vast majority of Christians are not prepared. They sit quietly and hope the conversation switches direction, or guiltily nod so they don't attract attention. Without knowledge of the evidence to support their faith, many become discouraged.

They become convinced by teachers like the famous atheist, Christopher Hitchens, who exclaimed, "That which can be asserted without evidence, can be dismissed without evidence." Hitchens clearly believed that the claims of Christianity have no evidence to back them up and therefore can be dismissed without thought. You will find in this book that his statement cuts both ways. We will put the claims of atheism to the test too, and you will get to make an educated decision on which side of the evidence you wish to be.

This study is the solution to bring your intellect and faith into alignment and create confidence and boldness in your daily walk. This study promises to help Christians regain that sense of integrity, peace and faith by wiping away the misperceptions that Christians have about scientific, historic and philosophical evidence. Whether you are a skeptic, an unsure Christian, or a sold-out evangelical, this study will embolden you in countless surprising ways. Through this study your eyes will be opened God's fingerprints on creation, life, Scripture and you!

Responsibility

> *"For since the creation of the world God's invisible qualities—his eternal power and divine nature—have been clearly seen, being understood from what has been made, so that people are without excuse." – Romans 1:20*

Paul says that "people are without excuse." People are responsible for their own decisions, so whether or not you are conflicted about the truth of Christianity, your decision with regard to Jesus Christ is your responsibility and the consequences of that decision are yours to bear. West Point understands the danger of excuses as well.

Our first act at West Point was obedience. An upperclassman in a crisp white and grey uniform pointed to the spot on which I was to stand. As I moved there and stood in what my high school mind imagined was the position of attention, I was put into the no-excuse

world. The first words out of the upperclassman's mouth as he looked at me from under the low brim of his hat were to explain to me that when addressed by an officer or upperclassman I was allowed only four responses, "Yes Sir," "No Sir," "No Excuse Sir," and "Sir I do not understand."

Can you imagine the audacity of West Point to take us young, intelligent, high-school graduates, bursting with potential and limit our universe of words to twelve? West Point had to cut us off from the relativism of our lives up to that point. They had to get us into a world of truth where anything but the truth was unacceptable, and that no excuse and no rationalization was good enough to depart from the truth. We were under strict oversight for our first year of school. We couldn't talk when outside, we walked at a hurried pace with head and eyes straight ahead, and we constantly had extra pieces of knowledge we had to master. If we were ever stopped by an upper classman or officer, we had to keep our four responses in mind.

West Point has become the embodiment of leadership through over two hundred years of history. It has produced an unmatched list of military, political and business leaders. There is a good reason why the very first thing they demand from its students is "no excuse." There is a purpose behind creating a full year of practical application where cadets are tested by that standard in every part of their conduct. Christians must develop the habit of honesty even under difficult circumstances. Consider then that when Paul says that "people are without excuse," he does so for a very good reason.

The purpose of not allowing excuses is to save your life. West Point focuses on battle and Paul focuses on eternity. Paul knows that those who do not accept Jesus Christ as their savior while living have an eternity in hell after death. For this study, you can tap into the no-excuse mindset and gain the insights that it allows. My perspective in writing this study is clear, but whether or not you decide for or against Jesus, you must do the work to evaluate the evidence and then take intelligent ownership of your decision.

Sam Harris, a leading atheist intellect wrote in his book, *Letter to a Christian Nation*, "I know of no society in human history that ever suffered because its people became too desirous of evidence in support of their core beliefs."[i]

CHAPTER 1

Truth

Does Truth Exist?

Possible Conclusions

> In each chapter the <u>Possible Conclusions</u> section states the possible conclusions that you might reach after studying the topic.

1. No, truth does not exist. We cannot know for sure what reality is. Scientific, historic and religious truths are out of our capacity to know.
2. Yes, truth exists. We can know the truth with perfection or with a high probability. Scientific, historic and religious truths can be determined through an examination of evidence.

Assessment

> In each chapter the <u>Assessment</u> section gives you the opportunity to see if you learned something as you read the chapter. You will answer the same questions before and after you have read the chapter. This is a powerful method for measuring learning in any environment.

Instructions: For each question circle Y/T or N/F. Circle Y/T if the question or statement is True or if the answer is Yes. Circle N/F if the question or statement is False or if the answer is No. Before you read the chapter, mark your answers in the "Before Reading" column and after you have read the chapter, mark your answers in the "After Reading" column.

Question	Before	After Reading

	Reading	
Do lies exist?	Y/T - N/F	Y/T - N/F
Can we really know that physical objects exist?	Y/T - N/F	Y/T - N/F
Can we really know what happened in the past?	Y/T - N/F	Y/T - N/F
Religions rely only on faith, and the truth about them cannot be known.	Y/T - N/F	Y/T - N/F
Truth is always in line with our desires.	Y/T - N/F	Y/T - N/F
Even if truth does not exist I can still do good things.	Y/T - N/F	Y/T - N/F

Truth Introduction

"Back up! Back up! Back up!" I yelled through the headset to my driver. I was standing up in the hatch through the top of the HMMWV behind the .50 Cal machine gun when I saw over the edge of the ravine that it was an enemy camp. That is when our backwards adventure began.

The Yakima, Washington training area is a desert, and the area over which we were attempting to drive was filled with large rocks. We bounced backwards as fast as we could, running over everything in our way. Fortunately, we got away and I was able to report the enemy location.

I spent several years in the army as the leader of scout platoons. I've been thrown around like a rag doll for hours with my body halfway out the top of HMMWVs as they bounced along rough terrain, and I've worn out more than one pair of boots walking to remote places so I could see what the enemy was up to. My units were the eyes on the ground and my higher leaders counted on us to report the truth of where we were and what we saw. We were the early warning system. Fortunately, I was never in combat, but for those in combat, if scouts fail to provide accurate, timely information, people die.

In battle, the Army spends a lot of time trying to determine the truth. We are constantly on the lookout for intelligence about the enemy and what they might do. Our leadership studies the history of our enemies to determine how they might act in the future. We put scouts in places so that they can report on enemy activities or the lack of activities so that we can predict their plan and are ready before they attack. We gather reports about the status of our own troops and equipment so we have the best possible understanding of what we are capable of doing and how we should arrange our forces.

We never doubted that truth existed. Even if we could not know the enemy's plan perfectly, we knew it existed. Even if our status on our own forces was not 100% accurate, we knew enough to organize properly. No one ever suggested that truth could not be known because our representation of it was not perfect. No one threw their helmet down and protested that they were not going to be involved in the fight because they did not know whether the enemy was located on Hill A or Hill B. Soldiers, like you, are in a battle whether you like it or not. Opting out because you can't know the truth with 100% certainty gets you killed.

Rest assured some things we knew were absolutely true. I used to tell my students that there are no soft spots on a tank, and if there were, when they fell, they would not hit one. One particular day, a senior NCO was a tank commander going through a live-fire shooting range. The tank commander's seat is inches to the right of the main gun, which recoils backward into the tank as it shoots. As the tank fired its 120mm gun, in a fraction of a second the recoil of the gun brushed his left arm, which was slightly beyond the safety cage. He felt the slight contact with his uniform and instantly fainted. He fell to the bottom of the tank like a limp noodle. There was no question in his mind that the gun tube was real.

Philosophical debate about the existence of truth can go on forever, and you can allow it to confuse you about your ability to know truth, or you can accept the plainness of it and move on. I have no doubt that if the philosophers Kant or Nietzsche were the tank commander that day, they'd be passed out on the tank floor too!

Exploring Truth

What is the most memorable lie you have ever told? What if I could explain to you that it was not really a lie? If there is no truth, there is no lie! Here's the logic behind that statement.

- A lie is something that is contrary to the truth. (Premise #1)
- Truth is an accurate representation of reality. (Premise #2)
- So if there is no truth (*an accurate representation of reality*), then there cannot be a lie. (Conclusion) You're off the hook!

We are on a quest for truth; the truth about truth and the truth about the most important questions in our lives and eternity. If we determine that truth does not exist, or that we cannot really know truth, then we have saved ourselves a whole bunch of time and we can stop now. You don't engage on a trip if you don't believe your destination doesn't exist. Who would set off on a journey to Gotham City or buy a ticket for a Chipmunks concert? No one would because they do not exist. If, however, truth does exist and we can know it, then we are on a journey that will change our lives.

In this study we will evaluate evidence that can guide us in answering some of the most troublesome and important questions of life and meaning. These are questions that have dogged mankind from the beginning of time, but you will see that in most cases things are not as complicated as you might think.

We use evidence to come to reasonable conclusions about the truth of reality. If we can't use evidence to come to some sort of conclusion because truth does not really exist, then the evidence is useless and so is our examination of it. For instance, if we were to take the time to examine very strong evidence that pertains to the creation of life, but we could not really rest comfortably choosing to believe that we were created by God or evolved from tadpoles, then does it even matter?

Is it possible to know logical truth?

Here is a simple logical exercise. Take the statement,

- "Truth either exists or it does not exist." Is that a true statement?
- Yes.
- Good. Problem solved. Logical Truth exists.

We will use logical arguments to bolt down our conclusions. Logical arguments are simply a way of organizing our evidence so that we can come to a reasonable conclusion. For example:

1. Christians believe that Jesus died for their sins. (Premise #1)
2. Joe is a Christian. (Premise #2)
3. Joe believes that Jesus died for his sins. (Conclusion)

If premises #1 and #2 are true then #3 is a valid conclusion. Said in another way, if the evidence supports that #1 is true and the evidence supports that #2 is true, then our conclusion is a reasonable conclusion.

This seems really obvious, but do not roll your eyes yet. Famous philosophers throughout history have debated whether or not truth exists, and many recent ones came to a conclusion that it does not. Those debates are responsible in large part for societies turning away from the pursuit of truth in exchange for the pursuit of pleasure. The rejection and overthinking a simple logical problem like the one we solved in 10 seconds is the foundation for much of the trouble we see in the world today. Let's face it, if truth does not exist, then we are faced with what to do next.

Truth often points us in a direction that is contrary to our desires. Let's face it, we are all battling the desire for things we want now verses the things that take time. For instance, it is true that if you save only $500/year for 25 years and get 7% interest per year, you will have invested $12,000 dollars but have $33,838 in the bank. Wouldn't it be great to have that much money? However, the latest phone, or dress is only $500 for a limited time and you want it now.

The battle between our immediate desires and truth encourages people to seek a loophole to truth. We might say things like, I can get another $500 to invest this year, or I could never come up with that amount of money every year, or 7% is not a realistic number. We can rationalize our unbeneficial actions in pursuit of our wants in many ways.

Some of the modern influential philosophers who have concluded that truth does not exist include:

- Friedrich Wilhelm Nietzsche (1844 - 1900) said, "There are no eternal facts, as there are no absolute truths." He was considered a strong atheist and famously claimed, "God is dead," and yet also worried that no God meant meaninglessness and confusion. *He suffered and died with a severe mental illness.*

- Immanuel Kant (1724 - 1804) wrote extensively about our inability to fully know the reality of even physical objects. My question to anyone accepting this philosophy is, *What would you make of the pen and paper he used to write his philosophy. Did he know that they were real?*

- Jacques Derrida (1930 - 2004), who was strongly influenced by Friedrich Nietzsche brought the meaning of words into question. My question to anyone accepting this philosophy is, *If the interpretation of words is left to each individual, then who could take his words seriously?*

Can you see why there might be confusion about truth for people who are relying on *authority figures* like these to come to a conclusion before deciding for themselves? I believe that you are fully capable of evaluating the evidence for yourself and coming to a reasonable conclusion. In fact, I say that if you do not deliberately evaluate and decide on your own, you have surrendered your intellect without a fight, and that would be the opposite of intelligent.

I believe that the most important decision you can make is the acceptance of Jesus' sacrifice for you on the cross, but that truly is a personal decision. No matter how many times you have gone to church or how long you have sung in the student choir or how devout your parents are, you must make that decision yourself. If you do not actively choose Christ, you have rejected Christ. There is no middle ground.

Is it possible to know physical truth?

The answer to this question seems incredibly simple regardless of how complicated Immanuel Kant made it. Here is a simple test to determine if you can know the reality of physical objects. Take your left hand and grab one finger from your right hand. Now pull backwards.

The question of truth sometimes gets bogged down in the seemingly *unknowable* facts of historical and religious beliefs.

I believe it is fair to say that logical truth exists and that we can rest assured that there is truth about physical objects such as the chair you are sitting on and the clothes that you have on, but what about historical truth and religious truth?

Is it possible to determine a historical truth?

What was the exact shade of George Washington's false teeth? We can never know the exact color of his teeth even if we went and dug them up? The condition of his teeth over the past 200 years would certainly have changed what they look like, and we do not know what he's been eating in Heaven. It would be fair to say that we can't determine that fact about history, but we can be certain that George Washington did live and that he did in fact have false teeth.

A great deal of historical fact can be known with near certainty based on the detail and number of documents written at the time of the event. We can be sure that the testimonies of eye witnesses are key to the credibility of historical events. Even though each person might see things differently, there are always key corroborations that validate the event. As an example, the history of 9/11 has been recorded through documents and personal memoirs. If you read the account of a witness who was inside of Tower 2 when the second plane hit, it would be dramatically different than a witness watching from the ground yet there would be major overlaps in time and descriptions of events that they both witnessed. There is no reason to believe that the multiple accounts of an event that happened in 2001 should be any more reliable than multiple accounts written about an event in 1776 or 33 AD.

Is it possible to determine a religious truth?

This is the question about which this entire study revolves. We know that Christianity is either true or it's not true. You will have to decide for yourself as the study goes on which stance you take. Can we be certain within a reasonable doubt that Christianity is true, that miracles have happened and that Jesus rose from the dead? We will explore those subjects along with whether or not moral values exist and whether or not a loving God could allow evil in the world.

Christianity, much more than any other religion sets itself up for success or failure based on the sheer number of scientific claims it makes and the amount of literature that presents itself as scripture. Scripture is a recording of historic events, so evidence can be used to evaluate its truthfulness. If there is any religion that is poised to be knocked off its high horse, it's Christianity. Paul said, in 1 Corinthians 15:14, "If Christ has not been raised, our preaching is useless and so is your faith." We must accept that if God did in fact create the Universe, all of the evidence will either point to that fact or at the very least not point away from it.

Evidence is how we are going to evaluate a truth from a lie, but remember that evidence is worthless if truth does not exist. Have you determined whether or not truth exists?

Even the Bible cannot rise above a determination that there is no truth. If there is no truth, the Bible becomes just another ancient novel. When there is no true standard for how to behave then we become our own standard. Paul tells us in Romans 1:24-25 that when "they exchanged the truth about God for a lie" that "God gave them over in the sinful desires of their hearts…" [ii]

Questions to Consider
- If there was no God looking down on you, and your parents, friends and teachers would never know what you did, and if there were no consequences for being completely selfish, how would you act?
- What if you were in a foreign country by yourself where no one knew you and you had a million dollars, what would you do?

Did you think about doing really nice things or selfish things with the time and money?

If there is no truth, then none of the things you thought about doing, whether selfless or selfish, are right or wrong. If you fed the hungry and housed the homeless – who cares? If you partied until dawn every day for a year and ended up broke – who cares? However, if truth exists, then how you use your money, time and talents matters very much.

Implications of Each Conclusion

> In each chapter the Implications of Each Conclusion section exposes the logical and/or implied characters of worldview according to each conclusion. The bottom line is that you cannot have it both ways. If you eliminate God from your belief system, there are certain liberties you have, but you cannot then invoke God for the things you like about God.

If you believe that there is no truth or that it is unknowable, then you are accepting the responsibility to do as you please in pursuit of whatever desire you have. There are no greater obligations or logical reasons to serve or sacrifice and even if you choose to do so, there is no value to it. There is no ultimate meaning, purpose or value to any act or to life itself.

If you believe that truth exists then you have a natural obligation to act in accordance with truth.

> In each chapter you should go back to the Assessment section and complete the After-Reading Column to see if you learned something as you read the chapter. You will answer the same questions that you answered before you read the chapter. This is a powerful method for measuring learning in any environment.

> Answer the Assessment questions from the beginning of the chapter again

> In each chapter the Characteristics section gives the logical and/or implied characteristics of the eternal power as it pertains to the subject of the chapter. The point is that without looking at the Bible, we can independently determine the characteristics of the creator and compare that with the Bible.

Characteristics of the Truth Giver
- Eternal
- Immaterial
- Unchanging

> In each chapter the <u>Deliverables</u> section summarizes key information found in the chapter.

Deliverables
- Truth either exists or it does not exist.
- Evidence can be evaluated to determine truth.
- Truth exists. Physical truth exists. Historical truth exists. Religious truth exists.
- If truth does not exist, there is no right or wrong, good or evil.
- Christ is the only way to God is an exclusive truth claim that is either true or it is not.
- Truths about Truth
  1. Truth accurately reflects reality. Truth is what describes reality properly.
  2. Truth is discovered. It's not invented. Truth exists independent of someone's knowledge of it. (Gravity existed prior to Newton)
  3. Truth is multicultural. It is the true for all people, in all places at all times. (2+2=4)
  4. Truth is unchanging. Our belief in truth may change, but truth does not. (Flat earth vs spherical earth.)
  5. Beliefs do not change facts no matter how sincerely they are held. (Sincerely believe that earth is flat, but does not change the truth.)
  6. Truth is independent of the demeanor of the person expressing it. (Just because an arrogant person expresses it, does not make the truth he says wrong. A humble person expressing a falsehood does not make it a truth.)

  All truths are absolute and exclusive.[iii]

CHAPTER 2

Something From Nothing

Can Something Come from Nothing for No Reason?

Possible Conclusions

1. Yes. By chance something can come into being from nothing. Not just something came into being, but the enormity of the Universe came into being from nothing.
2. No. Something cannot come into being from nothing without a cause. The cause of the Universe must have been all powerful and outside of time, space and matter.

Assessment

Question	Before Reading	After Reading
Small things can come into existence from nothing without a cause.	Y/T - N/F	Y/T - N/F
The Universe has existed forever.	Y/T - N/F	Y/T - N/F
Nothing = Something.	Y/T - N/F	Y/T - N/F
The Big Bang happened.	Y/T - N/F	Y/T - N/F
The Earth is 6,000 – 10,000 years old.	Y/T - N/F	Y/T - N/F

Something from Nothing Introduction

It got cold after the sun went down but there was still work to do. My HMMWV pulled off of the main road and in to a field that had been turned into a temporary command center. There were other vehicles parked off to the side and a group of dark-green Army tents stood straight to our front. We parked next to one of the other vehicles and I hopped out to locate the place I was supposed to be for the planning meeting.

The whole area was dark and quiet even though I knew that there were a lot of people around. I found the door to the Tactical Operations Center (TOC) and tried to go inside. The tent flaps overlapped three ways in order to block the light from inside getting out. Opening those flaps was like swimming in heavy canvas. Every time I tried to go into a tent like this I felt like I had awakened and was struggling with my sheets tightly wrapped around me. 'Let me in!' I thought.

Even though we were in the middle of the countryside near the Korean DMZ, the light and heat on the inside were a reminder of the comforts of civilization. The rooms of the tent were busy with activity and with men quickly marking up a large whiteboard. It was like the New York Stock Exchange trading floor in camo.

Our unit was in the middle of the planning process for a large attack on the enemy. The whiteboard had countless columns and rows for tracking all of the units, their status, strengths and locations. The meeting I was going to was one of the key events in the planning process for pushing information to the troops on the ground. The point in time that we were most concerned about was that moment when we first crossed into enemy territory. We had to be fully prepared and on time.

That one point in time when our forces crossed into enemy territory had to be synchronized in order for our plan to have the best chance of success. Our commanders had a purpose in how they arranged our forces, artillery firing onto specific targets, helicopters delivering infantrymen to precise locations, and tanks rolling across the line had to work together in order to achieve our objective. The support forces carrying food and ammunition and medical care were all included in these plans and were prepared to support when and where needed. Military plans are complex and they never occur without huge amounts of effort and thought towards a purpose.

Any planning process is just an example of what we can imagine God was doing prior to the creation of the Universe... unless you accept that the Universe happened by chance.

Exploring Something from Nothing

Can something actually come from nothing?
Consider a small ball bouncing down the road past you as you walk. Is it possible that ball popped out of nothing in the air behind you and fell to the ground bouncing down the road? I believe we can all agree with the laws of physics that say that is impossible. It would be counter intuitive and without merit to claim otherwise. Some natural cause must have been responsible not only for the original production of the ball in a factory somewhere, but also for the movement of the ball down the street.[iv] Would you argue that it came from nothing by chance? No. You would be called crazy and illogical because everything has a cause.

What if you got to the bottom of the hill where the ball stopped in the bushes and saw that the ball had become as large as a car? Would you then consider the possibility that the ball came into existence without explanation? Of course not. The size of an object does not change the demand for a reason for its existence. But what if the ball was the size of the Universe, would that make a difference?

What are the possible conclusions as to how something came from nothing?
Before we demand an explanation for *why* something came into being from nothing, let's cover some of the evidence surrounding the question of whether or not the Universe did have a beginning. There are only two real categories of thought about the origins of the Universe.
1. It has always been here, meaning that there was no beginning and that it has been here for an infinitely long time or
2. It had a beginning.

Take a moment and imagine infinity. Imagine an infinite number of marbles. If there were an infinite number of marbles how much space would they take up? Did you realize that there a limited number of atoms in the universe?[v]

Thinking about the existence of infinity is something that can keep you up at night. What if the Universe has been in existence for an infinite amount of time, how much energy would you expect to be left? Unless there is another infinite energy source mysteriously created along with the infinite Universe, like a clock winding down, or your coffee getting cold, the energy would have been used up by now.

Infinitely Old Universe

It is important to note that this first category of no-beginning does not fall into the field of science and never has. These theories are pure speculation and cannot be supported by any evidence or even tested.[vi] The three main theories are the multiple universes, the cosmic egg and the cyclic universe.

Multiple Universes (Multiverse)

The multiple universes theory says that there is somehow a process which has been going on forever by which universes pop into something out of nothing on a continuous basis and we are just one of those infinite numbers of universes. This one straddles the fence of a beginning and does not set itself up against the evidence that our own

universe had a beginning. This theory is popular right now because as you will find out in a later lesson, scientists believe that it can account for the improbability of the exquisitely fine-tuned

forces in our universe that allow for life. You see, they argue, that if there are an infinite number of other universes, there is a chance that one of them would have life-permitting forces and we just got phenomenally lucky to be in one of the ones that does.

Cosmic Egg

Or you may hear about the cosmic egg theory which imagines a static universe in an incredibly dense ball that sits forever...at least until it suddenly begins to expand into the universe we see today.

Cyclic Universe (Oscillating Universe)

Finally, we have the cyclic universe which imagines that the universe has forever been expanding and collapsing and expanding again. The theory says that the universe goes through cycles of stretching itself out until it collapses back on itself and then the momentum of its collapse carries the matter back in the opposite direction in a new expansion phase which is farther and farther each time.

Universe Beginning from Nothing. (The Singularity, The Big Bang, The Creation Event)

When Scientists are restricted to using evidence to come to come to conclusions about the origin of the universe, they have concluded that the Universe came into existence from nothing.

This theory of the origin of the universe from nothing is not an obscure theory held by men with grey beards and pointy hats with moons and stars on them. It is commonly called the Big Bang Theory. No. It was not named after the TV show. It is a theory supported by Einstein's Theory of General Relativity and the work of Edwin Hubble, the namesake of the Hubble Telescope, among other Nobel Prize winners.

Einstein's Theory of General Relativity says that time, space and matter must exist at one time and that none can exist without the other two. Even after Einstein realized that his theory demanded a beginning of the Universe he still believed that the Universe was infinitely old and unchanging. Einstein actually tried to cover up the implied beginning with a hypothetical fudge factor. However, as the scientific community began to work with his theories they started independently confirming that there was no escaping the beginning of the Universe. Einstein later called that fudge factor a monumental blunder.[vii] Those who believed in an infinitely old universe have been dealt a death blow by Einstein and other mathematical and philosophical realities.

It was a Belgian Priest and physics professor, Georges Lemaitre, who proposed in 1927 that if every part of the universe, is moving away from every other part of the universe, they are each traveling on a path. If you follow every path backward they will coincide at one place.[viii] Edwin Hubble later observed that all objects in space in every direction are moving away from each other. Space itself is expanding.

The implications of something coming from nothing are plain to everyone including the scientists who began discovering the evidence for the beginning back in the early 1900's. Something from nothing demands a creator that is greater than the time, space and matter that make up our Universe.

The creation of the Universe from Nothing, commonly called the Big Bang, is a theory so solidly grounded in evidence that even those scientists who have been trying to disprove the theory have come to a dead end. In order to avoid the implications of a beginning to the universe, these theorists tried to prove that the universe is infinite and eternal, that it had no beginning in time. These well-educated scientists started more in the arena of science fiction than science and they ultimately failed to pass mathematical and physics hurdles.

Cosmologist Alex Vilenkin has evaluated potential infinite Universe scenarios and come to the following conclusion:

> *But this quantum creation from "nothing" seems to avoid these questions. It has a nice mathematical description, not just words. There is an interesting thing, though; the description of the creation of the universe from nothing is given in terms of the laws of physics. That makes you wonder, where are these laws? If the laws describe the creation of the universe, that suggests they existed prior to the universe. The question that nobody has any idea how to address is where these laws come from and why these laws in particular? So there are a lot of mysteries to keep us working.*[ix]

Now think about the Big Bang – the creation event. Trust your common sense and experience. Trust that the men and women who study this event for a living, people who have more education that any 10 of us combined are swirling around the funnel of evidence and coming out the bottom to the same conclusion – the universe had a beginning.

What is eye opening is to watch some of these very intelligent, sincere people try to explain how something could have popped into existence out of nothing, uncaused. It's like watching a child with crumbs around his mouth and chocolate streaks on his shirt come up with an elaborate explanation for the disappearance of the cookies. The honest ones will at least start with "theoretically..."

Contortions

As an example of both confusion and contortions, Lawrence Krauss, a theoretical physicist published a book called *A Universe From Nothing: Why There is Something Rather Than Nothing.*[x] A fair reading of that title would suggest that in the book Krauss will explain how the Universe came from nothing. However, Krauss explains that the title was just a "hook" and if that "hook gets you into the book that is great." He later says that "the nature of 'nothing' had changed, that we have discovered that 'nothing' is almost everything and that it has properties."[xi] It is at this point where I need to point us back to the session on Truth. Nothing either is nothing  or it is something. Changing the definition of nothing to make it fit your argument seems disingenuous. If I handed you a bowl and said, "It's clean! There is nothing in it," would you ignore the crusty thing stuck to the bottom or would you ask me for another bowl?

More recently, highly intelligent scientists, looking at the incredible mathmatical makeup of everything in the Universe, have suggested that reality is very much like being in a computer game. Everything is digital. They say that we are in a computer simulation, that we can never know for sure, but the design of things lead them to that conclusion.[xii] They suggest that some far superior race of beings created this simulation for some reason. As you can tell, these people have left the field of science, preferring science-ficion instead.

The conclusion that Universe came into existence out of NOTHING is so well documented by evidence that science considers it a fact. At the beginning, there was no Universe. Time, space and matter did not exist. At the beginning, the Universe was so small that you could not see it with the most advanced microscope and is now so large that the most powerful telescope can only see a miniscule fraction of it.

Let me back up for a second. Though the scientific community considers the beginning of the Universe a fact, it can't accept it as a fact because the implications of a beginning point to a supernatural cause. Their search for the accidental cause of the Universe must go on and it is essential for them to convince those who are seeking truth that they have the ability to someday, somehow find the cause of the *accidental* Universe.

A Challenge to Christians

In the same way scientists desire to reject a supernatural cause for the Universe, many Christians desire to reject the Big Bang. Scientists are left with theoretical guesswork and Christians are left without the scientific evidence to support their creation story. Christians who can set aside their predisposition to a 6,000 – 10,000 year old Universe and accept the scientific evidence that supports the Bible's creation narrative win. We can arm wrestle about the age of the universe, but let's not set our intellect aside and walk around with the self-imposed hypocrisy that we discussed in the Truth session. Let's accept the best proof that we have for our Creator.

A Warning on Evolution

Some of you may argue that if we are going to accept the scientific evidence for the Big Bang then we have to accept the scientific evidence for the theory of Evolution. We have a full session on the theory of Evolution, but there are two points that I will make here.

1. As Christians, we should evaluate all scientific, historic and philosophical evidence. *We should only accept valid evidence.* You will find that the *evidence* for the theory of Evolution is not valid.

2. At the 2014 *Defending Your Faith* conference Dr. Stephen C. Meyer, the author of *Signature in the Cell,* put it this way when asked if God could have directed evolution, "Why would you accept a theory that has absolutely no evidence to support it?"[xiii]

Implications of Each Conclusion

Believing that something came from nothing by chance is a position that ascribes supernatural affects to natural forces. It defers any answer as to why something came from nothing to some improbable far-future point when scientists become advanced enough to understand how something came from nothing uncaused even though that is logically, mathematically and physically impossible. The effect of denying any creator is to also deny any purpose. Natural forces, no matter how beautiful, cannot create purpose or meaning. If the universe, and in turn you are the result of chance, then all value we try to give life is just an illusion.

Believing that something came from nothing as the result of the will of God creates an obligation to seek the purpose of God's act of creation. It does not make any sense to accept the benefit of God's work without regard for why he provided it to us. Ignorance of God's purpose cannot be an excuse for living apart from God when he has also provided insight through his written testimony we call The Bible. We will tackle whether or not Scripture is reliable in a future lesson, but even if it did not exist, a reasonable person would seek to find the definite purpose in life if they believed that God created them. Interestingly, that is exactly what skeptics naturally attempt to do in spite of the "no-purpose" implications of their decision.

> Answer the Assessment questions from the
> beginning of the chapter again

Characteristics of the Creator of the Universe
- All Powerful
- Outside of time – Eternal
- Outside of Space
- Immaterial
- Purposeful

Deliverables
- Matter does not pop into being, from nothing, uncaused.
- All Infinite-Universe Theories are proven false.
    - The Multiple Universe (multi-verse), cosmic egg and Cyclic Universe theories are not viable.
- Infinity is impossible.

- If something never starts how can it get here?
- An infinitely old Universe would have no energy left.
- Science, math and philosophy have forced the belief in the Big Bang Theory; something from nothing.
- This theory demands a creator.
- Christians need not struggle with the Young-Earth theory. Accept valid evidence for our Creator and discuss the theology of the Young Earth amongst ourselves.

CHAPTER 3

Fine Tuning

Could Multiple, Extraordinarily Precise Life-Permitting Forces Happen by Chance from the Instant of Creation?

Possible Conclusions

1. Yes. Anything is possible no matter how improbable. By pure chance, the numerous, independent values of the forces of physics are the precise values necessary for life to exist.
2. No. There was a design in the creation from the beginning. The designer set these forces in order to make possible the lives he planned.

Assessment

Question	Before Reading	After Reading
I have no idea what fine tuning is.	Y/T - N/F	Y/T - N/F
No event, no matter how improbable, is really impossible.	Y/T - N/F	Y/T - N/F
Life exists, so we should not be surprised that physical forces have values that support life.	Y/T - N/F	Y/T - N/F
Most universes do not have forces that allow for life.	Y/T - N/F	Y/T - N/F
It is possible to prove the existence of other universes.	Y/T - N/F	Y/T - N/F

Physical forces can have a wide range of values that are compatible with life.	Y/T - N/F	Y/T - N/F

Fine Tuning Introduction

It was dark, really dark. No moon, no stars. In Army Ranger school we did most of our operations at night. And usually in Georgia or Florida we were in the middle of the woods. It was not uncommon for us to finish our mission at 1 o'clock in the morning and then start a couple hour walk towards our patrol base where we would be able to sleep for a couple of hours before starting again. On this night I was the radio operator. That meant I was responsible for carrying the radio and keeping it on the right frequency. Each person in the chain of command had their own frequency so if we wanted to talk to the commander we would have to be on his frequency, and if we wanted to the First Sergeant we would have to be on his frequency.

We had stopped for a moment and took a knee. I set my knee quietly into the wet leaves. The patrol leader ran to me and told me that we had to get our fire support officer on the line immediately. Unfortunately, my radio had slipped down into my ruck sack and was buried beneath a myriad of things that if I tried to remove would explode onto the ground around me. I could not see the dial and I could not use a flashlight since we were on a mission. In my head I worked out the difference between the frequency I was on and the one that I needed to be on. I was forced to try the change blindly. If I was unable to find the right frequency quickly, our mission would fail and so would our leaders. That may very well have been the difference between them passing Ranger School or getting kicked out.

The ranger instructor was standing over me, bearing down on me with an unseen pressure that any kid who has tried to do something stressful with their parent looking over their shoulder would understand. I felt the knob, which I was pretty sure was the right one and turned it in the direction that I thought it should go. 'Have I never done this in the dark before?' I chided myself. 'I've done this a million times during the day, how can I not be sure which knob is which?!' The entire time I acted as if I

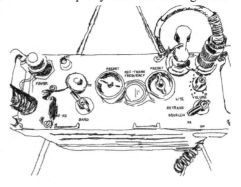

36

had everything under control. My stomach was in knots and I was hoping beyond hope to have good enough luck to get it right.

I felt the click-click-click-click-click-click-click-click-click-click-click-click-click-click-click-click... 'Sixteen clicks. That should be it,' I thought.

I pulled my hand out, put the hand mic up to my mouth and squeezed the push-to-talk button.

"Romeo Three-four, Romeo Three-four, this is X-ray two-eight over." A long silence of five seconds followed. My heart pounded.

I repeated, "Romeo Three-four, Romeo Three-four, this is X-ray two-eight over."

Each second poked me with the realization that I was going to have to confess my failure, then the radio sounded.

"X-ray two-eight this is Romeo Three-four, over."

I DID IT! I accepted that small salvation without a reaction and the mission continued. Like a car accident narrowly avoided, the world went on without taking notice. I handed the mic to the patrol leader.

In that situation, since I knew what frequency I was on and which one I needed to get to, I had a reasonable chance of getting the frequency I wanted. However, since I was not sure of which dial to use or how much each click changed the frequency, I was really in the dark. I had about a 1/100 (1%) chance of reaching the right frequency and pulling my bacon out of the fire. Those are not the odds I would want if I was trying to beat a train to the intersection, but they were not bad considering that there are 920 possible frequencies on the PRC-77 radio dial.

The existence of life-compatible laws of physics in Universe is highly improbable too, but to a much greater degree. The odds against a life-permitting Universe are much more like having a dial with tens of billions of possible frequencies and not knowing which one you are trying to get to.

What if the enemy stood our patrol leader against the wall with a rifleman pointing his weapon at him under threat of death if I did not get the right frequency? What if, the enemy didn't tell me which frequency was right? I heard him click off his safety and take aim. I reached my hand down into the bag and before turning the knob I began to think – of something – of some way out, but there was none. I just had to take a chance and pray.

Click-click-click-click-click-click-click-click-click-click-click-click-click-click-click-click... 'How many clicks do I do? Does it matter?' I thought. They all have an equal chance, 1/920. I stopped and prayed before pressing the push to talk button.

I spoke into the handset, "Romeo Three-four, Romeo Three-four, this is X-ray two-eight over." ...silence.

Again. "Romeo Three-four, Romeo Three-four, this is X-ray two-eight over."

Then the response, "Roger X-ray two-eight, this is Romeo Three-four."

I saw the rifleman engage his safety and lower his weapon. An amazing turn of events! By total chance I had found the right frequency.

What we will learn in today's study is that the entire Universe was against the wall under threat of death if certain forces were not on the precise frequency.

Exploring Fine Tuning

Nothing is Impossible

An NBA player makes on average 8 out of 10 free throws.[xiv] They make an average of 4 out of 10 from the three point line, and only 2 out of 10 from farther out.[xv] At what point do the odds become impossible? What if the odds were 1/1,000 that they could make a shot from across the court? Still possible? Yes.

But what if the odds were 1/10,000,000 that a player could make a shot from three miles away? When people determine highly-improbable odds like this they are imagining that nothing is impossible under the perfect conditions. They ask questions such as, "What if the environmental conditions were just right? What if there was a powerful updraft that carried the ball into the air and at the right point near the basketball court a swirling of the wind dropped the ball into the net? It's not impossible." They say, "pure chance could account for the occurrence of highly-highly-improbable events."

Does that make any sense to you?

What you will see in percent chances like this is a belief that very few things are really impossible when conditions are just right. Even though it defies common sense and we can't imagine something like that happening in 1,000,000,000 tries, it does not matter to people who will say, "Well the chance is still not 0%."

Probabilities mean something when they refer to something that is physically possible. However, when the probability relies on multiple physical forces acting in perfect harmony at the proper times, directions and energy, the legitimate disbelief in even the possibility of the event occurring is warranted. A basketball player throwing a basketball at the edge of his range is improbable, but not impossible. A player outside of his range having to bounce it into the basket becomes even more unlikely, but even then there is only one added variable. When the player is far outside of his range and other random forces have to assist, we can rightly say that it is impossible, even if someone applies probabilities to it happening.

Fine Tuned for Life

Fine Tuning refers to the set of forces in the Universe that are precisely the right value for permitting life. There are a number of these forces, that if they were changed by the tiniest amount, the Universe would not allow life to exist. In most cases, if these forces were different, atoms could not form and the Universe would not allow for planets and galaxies and solar systems to form, let alone life. In some cases the gravity would be so great that the mass of the Universe would never be able to escape its force and in other cases the attraction of particles to each other would not be strong enough to allow atoms to form. Either way, no life.

There is no debate as to whether or not these forces exist or how precise they are. What is at question is the explanation as to how the forces came to be so finely tuned. Either they came to be this way by chance or they were set by a designer. It will be helpful to walk through a couple of examples so you can understand the full situation.

Let's first relate fine tuning to the radio frequency I was trying to find on my mission. I had better than one chance in 920 (9.2×10^2) to get the right frequency. Those are tough odds, but gravity had one chance in 10^{60} (10 with 60 zeros after it) to be at the perfect value. (See end of chapter for illustration on exponential numbers) That is a lot of clicks of the dial.[xvi] One argument says that pure chance reached its hand down into the ruck sack and without knowing which frequency was needed, and having no preference of one over another, luckily picked its value. The other argument says that it was dialed by a creator who planned life.

If you knew what numbers were going to be drawn for the next lottery would you pick them? Of course you would. You would purposely select the right numbers in order to win millions of dollars. You wanted to win. What was the purpose of getting the life-permitting forces exactly right? If there is a designer, he picked the numbers knowing what he had planned.

There was a recent lottery drawing where the winner received $1.59 Billion.[xvii] If you had a ticket in that lottery, your chances of winning were one in 292,201,338 (2.9 x 10[8]). [xviii] That is a small chance, but you were 3.42 x 10^{50} times ***more*** likely to win that lottery than the exact right value of the gravitational constant happening by chance. These numbers are so massive that they are really impossible to image so let's try a visual. You are many times more likely to randomly pick a pre-identified, specific grain of sand from among the worlds' beaches and deserts than the exact right value for gravity happening by chance.[xix] What if the consequence for picking the wrong grain of sand is that there would be no life? And what if you do not get a second try?!

Here's what I would do if given that challenge. I would find the nicest beach in the world and kick my feet up and make excuses as to why I could not pick yet.

When fine tuning is taken together with our next lesson

which will cover the improbability of life coming about by chance it seems as if the Universe was created with life permitting values so that life could exist. There seems to be a purpose to the design.

> *We are, by astronomical standards, a pampered, cosseted, cherished group of creatures... If the Universe had not been made with the most exacting precision we could never have come into existence. It is my view that these circumstances indicate the universe was created for man to live* in.[xx] *– John O'Keefe, NASA Astronomer*

A comparison of consequences of failure might be made to the program we have on earth called the Search for Extra Terrestrial Intelligence, (SETI). The program has been around since 1984 and has scoured the radio frequencies of the Universe day and night for years for some possible indication of life beyond our planet. "Currently the Center for SETI Research develops signal-processing technology and uses it to search for signals from advanced technological civilizations in our galaxy."[xxi]

All of this effort and expense has been made on the highly improbable chance that ET life exists. It is not as if we know that there is life out there. The entire thing may be a total waste of money and resources. What if SETI was told at the beginning of their grand work that they had to choose to listen to only one frequency randomly pulled from a hat? They then had one chance to tune in and listen to that frequency, and that if they did not hear anything then the whole program would be scrapped and never resumed. That ultimatum would be absurd, yet the one-chance-to-get-it-right was what came with the beginning of the Universe. The constants that allow for life had to be right – right from the beginning. There were no redos, no erasers, no knobs to turn the heat up a bit. There was one chance to get the forces exactly right otherwise life would not be possible.

Mankind or ....

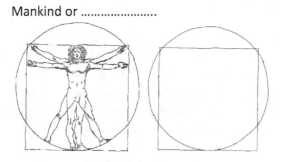

This is the random-chance position of how these forces came to be, but without the benefit or hope of even knowing what life was. These were totally random values set in place for no reason and without a care for what may come next. If SETI did not hear anything would anyone be surprised? No. Of course not. But, what if they did hear signs of life from that one frequency? Would that be an indicator to you that they were peeking when they picked from the hat and that they already knew that life existed at that frequency?

Somehow, the Universe is perfectly dialed in. These values had one shot to get it right, and to add emphasis, they accompanied the formation of the Universe. They were not figured out somehow after everything got started.

Here is what we know so far. There is only one universe that had a beginning from nothing at some point in the past. Along with the time, space and matter that came into existence, there were the laws of physics that accompanied the creation and dictate how the components of the Universe react to each other. Think of these laws like the cream in your coffee. They permeate everything. Think of them as the laws of our country. They are not anything physical, but they dictate the standards of how we treat each other. Those forces of physics are incredibly fine-tuned to allow for life.

A Basket Full

Now hold onto your hats because we have only talked about one – ONE – finely-tuned value. Dr. Hugh Ross has identified over 140 such cosmic values that must be precise in order for life to exist. A few of the other major ones include:[xxii]

- The Cosmological Constant, which dictates how quickly the Universe is expanding, is fine tuned to one part in 10^{120}. [xxiii]
- The Weak Force, which is works inside atoms is fine tuned to one part in 10^{100}. [xxiv]
- The Expansion Rate of the universe one second after the creation event is fine tuned to one part in "one hundred thousand million million" according to Stephen Hawking. [xxv]
- The density of the universe at 10^{-43} seconds after the creation event was fine tuned to one part in 10^{60}. [xxvi]

What should become apparent at this point is that we are not looking at one stand-alone force that somehow miraculously got it right. No, we are seeing a long set of forces that got it exactly right. If any of them had been off by the tiniest amount, life would not be here. This is like a set of 140 radios, all randomly set to different frequencies from among hundreds and hundreds of billions of choices at the same time and each one getting it exactly right. Try balancing 140 toothpicks end to end on top of each other.

> *A common sense interpretation of the facts suggests that a superintellect has monkeyed with physics, as well as with chemistry and biology, and that there are no blind forces worth speaking about in nature. The numbers one calculates from the facts seem to me so overwhelming as to put this conclusion almost beyond question.* – Fred Hoyle, British Astrophysicist[xxvii]

The fact of the fine-tuning of the Universe to allow for life begs us to wonder how it came to be this way. Those who point to God as the creator have a pretty easy time accepting these facts, while those who will look for natural causes to everything we see will take the stance that there is no way for us to know the answer. The scientific approach has left the bounds of what can be proven scientifically and have begun to explore extra-scientific theories such as the multi-verse and 'we are living in a computer simulation' in order to maintain the *plausibility* of natural causes (chance) as the cause of the fine tuning. They have walked through the end zone, out the other side and are yelling for the quarterback to throw them the ball.

Though the multi-verse has been disproven mathematically and philosophically, scientists continue to see this as their last best option for carrying on the conversation about the choice between chance and design. You see, if there are an infinite number of universes out there, then the fact that we are existing in one of the tiny number that have values that allow for life should not be surprising.

Harry Cliff, the First Science Museum Fellow at University of Cambridge summarizes the situation well in his 2015 discussion about two other fine-tuned forces;

> *We live in one of the places in the multiverse where the two numbers are just right. We live in a Goldilocks universe. Now, this idea is extremely controversial, and it's easy to see why. If we follow this line of thinking, then we will never be able to answer the question, "Why is there something rather*

> *than nothing?" In most of the multiverse, there is*
> *nothing, and we live in one of the few places where*
> *the laws of physics allow there to be something. Even*
> *worse, we can't test the idea of the multiverse. We*
> *can't access these other universes, so there is no way*
> *of knowing whether they're there or not.*[xxviii]

You should have enough evidence to come to a reasonable conclusion about the origin of the fine tuning of the Universe. If you are not sure which way or the other is more reasonable, you can do what I do when I am undecided. "I do not know, but if I had to bet my left arm, I would say that _____ was correct."

Implications of Each Conclusion

Believing that the 140 independently fine-tuned values of the forces of physics necessary for life to exist happened by chance is to accept that science can no longer provide you answers in this area. It is possible at this point to pick whichever theory best suits you since none will have, nor can they have, any additional empirical verification or contradiction. The effect of denying any creator is to also deny any purpose. Natural forces, no matter how beautiful, cannot create purpose or meaning. If the fine-tuned universe, and in turn you, are the result of chance, then all value we try to give life is just an illusion.

Believing that the Universe is fine tuned for life as the result of the will of God creates an obligation to seek the purpose of God's act of creation. It does not make any sense to accept the benefit of God's work without regard for why he provided it to us. Ignorance of God's purpose cannot be an excuse for living apart from God when he has also provided insight through his written testimony we call The Bible. We will tackle whether or not Scripture is reliable in a future lesson, but even if it did not exist, a reasonable person would seek to find the definite purpose in life if they believed that God created them. Interestingly, that is exactly what skeptics naturally attempt to do in spite of the "no-purpose" implications of their decision.

Answer the Assessment questions from the
beginning of the chapter again

Characteristics of the Fine Tuner

- Purposeful
- Outside of time – Eternal
- All Powerful
- Outside of Space
- Immaterial
- Perfect

Deliverables

- There are 140 cosmic values that must be precise for life to exist in the Universe.
- The forces did not have to be the values that they are.
- They were put in at the creation of the Universe.
- Gravity is fine tuned to one part in 10^{60}. That is 10 with 60 zeros after it.
- This design has forced atheists to adopt the multiple-universe or 'we are living in a computer simulation' theories, which are proven false, in order to allow for the chance of chance.

Special Section on Exponential Numbers

The exponential numbers that scientists use in determining the probabilities for certain events or the quantity of different things can be mind-blowingly small or large. For instance, the chance of the value of gravity being the exact value that it needs to be is 1 part in 10^{60}. That's really small, but who can even imagine that. Even when I talk about the chance of you winning the billion-dollar lottery being 1 chance in 2.9×10^8, the number is so small as to be insignificant. But here's where it gets really confusing, the exponent 60 is 7.5 times bigger than the exponent 8. How then is the number 10^{60}, 3.42×10^{50} times larger than 2.9×10^8?

The key take away from this section is that every 1 increase in exponential value multiplies the value by 10 times.

Here is a simple graphic example using the number 10 as the base. See at the bottom how it becomes ten times less of a percentage for every 1 increase in exponential.

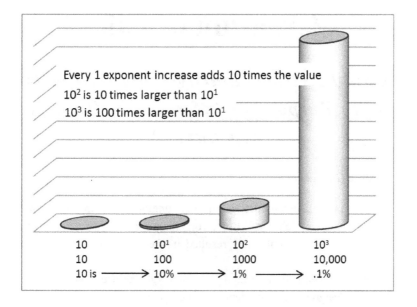

Every 1 exponent increase adds 10 times the value

10^2 is 10 times larger than 10^1

10^3 is 100 times larger than 10^1

10	10^1	10^2	10^3
10	100	1000	10,000
10 is ⟶ 10% ⟶		1% ⟶	.1%

CHAPTER 4

Creation of Life

Could Extraordinarily Complex Codes With Purposeful Information Happen by Chance?

Possible Conclusions

1. Yes. Inanimate material, through unguided circumstances over long periods of time, organized into ever increasing complexity until they resulted in the first self-sustaining life form.
2. No. Complex information cannot organize itself. The intricate design of life is evidence of a designer.

Assessment

Question	Before Reading	After Reading
Life started from non-living chemicals.	Y/T - N/F	Y/T - N/F
When left alone, non-living things sometimes get more organized.	Y/T - N/F	Y/T - N/F
Artificial intelligence (AI) has developed consciousness.	Y/T - N/F	Y/T - N/F
Biologists work according to the belief that life only comes from life.	Y/T - N/F	Y/T - N/F
DNA is a simple molecule.	Y/T - N/F	Y/T - N/F
Scientists have observed life coming from non-living molecules.	Y/T - N/F	Y/T - N/F

Creation of Life Introduction

Then he did it. It all happened in slow motion and though we were leaning forward in our seats trying to somehow prevent the approaching collision, my Lieutenant friend carried on with his explanation to the General.

"Well sir, we had certain unavoidable situations that pushed back our progress, but we are really on track to get the entire job done on time and with excellent proficiency," he said. The General sat back in his seat, took off his glasses and placed them on the open notebook in front of him.

Lieutenant Marshall continued, "So in three months...."

The General cut him off, "Stop. Please – for a second. I do not want to move on until I have a better understanding of how you got into the situation you are in right now."

This was the disaster that the Lieutenant had walked into and there was no escape now. The General proceeded to drag the poor Lieutenant through every one of his equivocations, selective truths, justifications, rationalizations and fuzzy statements. It was painful to watch, but instructive for dealing with the reality of tough situations.

The General already knew the answer to the question before he asked it. He was testing the character of my friend to see if he could overcome his desire to look perfect in front of the General and simply lay out the situation as it was. Unfortunately, the Lieutenant did what we call a hand-wave. If you can imagine someone waving their hand in a big rainbow-like arc while trying to brush past a question that they do not  want to answer, you will get the idea. The hand-wave is often used when a senior Army officer asks a junior officer where they are on the map. The junior officer, not having a clue, unfolds the map on the hood of a HUMMW-V and says, "Right here," as his index finger quickly makes an airplane-like landing and takeoff over an area the size of New York City.

That is a hand wave! When you try to look smart but have no facts.

Watch for hand waves when dealing with the difficult questions of how life could have developed from non-life. Watch for it in every circumstance. Hand waves are nearly always accompanied by wishy-washy, non-specific language. Character issues are revealed when the hand-wave commences, and the speaker then jumps to specific conclusions that are not supported and usually contradicted by the facts.

Exploring the Creation of Life

Chance or Design

Chance has been the alternative conclusion to design in our lessons on Creation and Fine-Tuning and we face the same decision today in regard to the origin of life. To summarize our possible conclusions, there are those who believe that in spite of essentially zero probability, chance is the best explanation for the Universe coming into existence and for the values of the physical constants being perfectly fine tuned to allow for life. The alternative explanation is that a power outside of time, space and matter designed and created everything for a purpose. Today we will look at another set of evidences revolving around the origin of life to determine what is the best possible explanation, chance or design.

Warning: Hand waves follow;

> *"The amazing thing is that every atom in your body came from a star that exploded. And, the atoms in your left hand probably came from a different star than your right hand. It really is the most poetic thing I know about physics: You are all stardust. You could not be here if stars hadn't exploded, because the elements - the carbon, nitrogen, oxygen, iron, all the things that matter for evolution - were not created at the beginning of time. They were created in the nuclear furnaces of stars, and the only way they could get into your body is if those stars were kind enough to explode. So, forget Jesus. The stars died so that you could be here today."*
> — *Lawrence M. Krauss*[xxix]

Life from Non-Life

The beginning of life from non-life is called abiogenesis. A-BIO-GENESIS, meaning without-life-beginning. This theory claims that from the chemical compounds formed along with the development of the Earth, there were conditions that fostered the unguided combining and recombining of these chemicals into what became some sort of self-replicating molecule. That molecule became increasingly complex over time to become a simple protein and the protein developed into DNA, which is the code for life held in every cell of every living organism. (There are abundant theories that attempt to explain the different paths from non-life to life.)

Evolutionary biologists do not know how this process happened and have no viable means for theorizing or recreating such an environment. Every closely-controlled experiment to reproduce such a beginning to life has completely failed.

Assuming Away Science

There is one gigantic assumption in theorizing that life arose from the random interactions of basic chemical elements. Anyone believing this theory must deny the law of entropy (the 2nd law of thermodynamics). Simply put, this law states that when left to themselves systems always move from order to disorder and higher heat to lower heat to a point of equilibrium. For example, the Universe is a closed system, that if left to itself will ultimately disperse all of its energy and die a frozen, dark death.

Anyone who has driven down country roads knows the natural effects of entropy. We have several large barns in our area that were once beautifully built and which are now collapsed and look as if they are on their knees and begging for water. One of our neighbors parked a car in his driveway in the 1990's and left it there. You can imagine what that looked like before it was finally towed away a couple of years ago; flat tires, faded and patchy paint on the hood, torn and missing vinyl on the roof, and a bushy vine eating it alive. Barns and cars naturally breakdown, they don't improve on their own. Would anyone park their car for a year and expect to come back to see it freshly polished and with a full tank of gas?

For people to make an assumption that suspends the laws of physics in order to allow for a theory to become viable is to sacrifice the laws of physics that they would otherwise defend to the death. Christians who feel compelled to assume away what the Bible says in order to accept a certain theory suffer from the same hypocrisy. If a Christian were to propose that the Bible does not really say that God created life in order to accept the theory of abiogenesis and evolution have sacrificed the theology that they would otherwise defend to the death. I strongly encourage consistency with whatever your view. One is truth and the other is not.

The law of biogenesis (from life beginning) is a cousin to the law of entropy and one that is equally assumed away by those wishing for abiogenesis to be true. The law of biogenesis says that life only comes from life. It is an accepted truth among scientists in the study of biology, including the study of evolution.

Ignoring these two fundamental laws of science while still attempting to prove a scientific theory seems ironic. This argument is like people in a basement arguing that there is in fact a 100th floor to the building while denying the first 99.

Chemicals or Consciousness

Are you just chemicals? If you are, what do you make of your personality, your thoughts, and your emotions? Whether or not you believe you have a soul, we each have these other non-physical, but very real attributes. Scientists do not attempt to answer this question because the development of self-consciousness is beyond the scope of scientific capabilities to determine.

Any scientific research into the development of the first life is simply a look into the possibilities of whether or not chemicals could randomly form into self-replicating chemicals and then become more ordered and complex over time. If we are talking about simple chemical processes, then consciousness never comes into play. No one would predict that any group of chemicals, no matter how complex, would be conscious. However, since consciousness exists it cannot be explained through natural causes.

Artificial Intelligence[xxx]

The world is very worried about the development of artificial intelligence and robots. It is very troublesome to believe that robots could develop to a point where they are self-replicating and capable of surviving without human intervention. The doomsday storyline goes something like this.

1. Robots are programed with artificial intelligence that allows them to learn on their own.
2. Robots decide that humans are dangerous to the survival of the planet.
3. Robots destroy the human race and *live* happily ever after.

The advance of artificial intelligence over the past decade has been impressive, but rest assured no matter how smart or self-sufficient robots become, they will never be alive. In fact, the distance between the smartest computers and the simplest life forms will always be  unbridgeable. A computer or a robot will never be alive.

Robots are like humans in the sense that their components are made up of chemicals and they are made to move like humans, but those chemicals are not alive and there is no scientist who would argue that someday they would become self-aware. This then demands the answers to hundreds of questions, not the least of which are:

1. How did chemicals become self-replicating on their own?
2. How did consciousness enter into a chemical equation?

Environment

The chemistry that everyone has to start with is the amino acid. Think of amino acids like the letters in the alphabet. We link letters (amino acids) together to form sentences which have a specific meaning. DNA in our cells link amino acids together to form proteins, which have specific jobs within our bodies. If I was to spell STOP, POST, you would drive into the intersection and cause an accident. POST does not mean anything, but STOP does.

Imagine if the word for STOP was 300 characters long. That is the average number of amino acids that have to form together in precise order in order for the protein to perform its job correctly in E-coli bacteria.[xxxi] Now imagine that the E-coli has about 2,900 different types

of proteins in it, each doing a different job.[xxxii] The E-coli, just like all living things, is like a bustling city with people, materials and vehicles travelling in different directions, busy doing their small part to make the city run. The odds against such a one-celled organism forming by chance are astronomical.

However, even before getting to the design and complexity that we see today, scientists attempting to prove the viability of abiogenesis have been thwarted by the incompatible composition of the early earth. The physical barriers to the building of ever increasing chemical complexity towards life are not small ones.

Oxygen itself turns out to be a leading cause of the failure of the theory. The earth has always had oxygen present in its atmosphere, so it would be impossible for the building blocks of life, amino acids, to survive without being oxidized.[xxxiii] The long strings of ordered and shaped amino acids that form proteins would have been destroyed in the presence of oxygen. Not one of the 2,000 proteins that form an amoeba could form. No life.

Think of a group of blindfolded kids holding their breath and sinking to the bottom of a swimming pool trying to hold hands and stretch from one end of the pool to the other. How long would you be able to attempt the feat? The incompatible environment would destroy your ability to connect. We find the same thing with amino acids and the proteins that they form. Even if amino acids were able to join together in the environment, they tend to break down in nature instead of remaining linked.

Chicken or the Egg?

DNA or the protein? DNA is the code that directs the production of proteins. It seems counterintuitive to suggest that simple, self-replicating proteins became more and more complex until they then formed a separate structure called DNA to take over the process. This theory must say that there was a random formation of proteins whose only job was to build DNA so that the DNA could then build proteins. This seems akin to building a car while you are jogging so that you can get to your destination faster, yet you do not know how to build a car and you do not know where you are going. The intellectual gymnastics necessary to connect chemicals to proteins to DNA seem impossible to perform, no matter how small the increments.

Information

The DNA in the simplest of organisms produces thousands of different types of proteins for very specific jobs in order to maintain the health of the organism. DNA is the foreman of the cellular world. The DNA in one of your cells has the same amount of information as that contained in about 4,000 books.[xxxiv] The DNA reads from those *books* millions of times a second and directs specific actions that maintain your life. The question of how meaningful, specific information is created is central to us coming to a conclusion as to how life began.

Implications of Each Conclusion

Believing that life sprung from non-life is to acknowledge that the laws of physics and biology have to be set aside from the outset. It is to claim that in spite of incompatible conditions, impossible odds and no evidence, something that looks specifically designed was actually the byproduct of time and material. You are accepting that you are an unintended accident without value greater than a dog or a rock and with no real purpose. Those suffering from low self-esteem and low-personal value are perfectly justified under this belief.

Believing that life was the result of the will of God creates an obligation to seek the purpose of God's act of creating life. You are saying that God created your life and that he did not do it by accident. A reasonable person would seek to find the definite purpose in life if they believed that God created them. Ignorance of God's purpose cannot be an excuse for living apart from God when he has also provided insight through his written testimony we call The Bible.

> Answer the Assessment questions from the
> beginning of the chapter again

Characteristics of the Life Giver
- Powerful
- Personal
- Purposeful

Deliverables
- The simplest components of life show an extraordinarily complex design. They are filled with purposeful information
- A-Bio-Genesis is the study of life springing from non-life
- Current biological science sticks to the law of Bio-Genesis. Life only comes from life.
- The Law of Entropy (The 2nd Law of Thermodynamics) says that when left to themselves systems always move from order to disorder and higher heat to lower heat to a point of equilibrium.
- Consciousness cannot be explained by chemicals.
- The DNA in one of your cells has the same amount of information as that contained in about 4,000 books
- DNA directs the production of proteins and some proteins build DNA. They had to be created at the same time.

CHAPTER 5

Evolution of Life

Can extraordinarily complex codes with purposeful information increase in complexity by chance over time?

Possible Conclusions

1. Yes. The first sustainable lifeform reproduced and through unguided circumstances over long periods of time, organized into ever increasing complexity resulting in life as we see it today.
2. No. Complex information cannot organize itself. The intricate design of life is evidence of a designer.

Assessment

Question	Before Reading	After Reading
Evolution is proven scientifically.	Y/T - N/F	Y/T - N/F
The fossil record shows the progression of evolution from simple to complex life over time.	Y/T - N/F	Y/T - N/F
The earliest fossils show extremely simple and primitive design.	Y/T - N/F	Y/T - N/F
DNA gains complexity from one generation to the next.	Y/T - N/F	Y/T - N/F
Sometimes evolution happens very quickly.	Y/T - N/F	Y/T - N/F

Evolution of Life Introduction

Rachel was a young wife with four children and one on the way. She homeschooled her children and styled hair part-time from her home in order to earn extra money. Her life had normal struggles and enjoyments until the day she found out that her husband had been cheating on her. Until that day, it was common for her and my wife to chat on the phone or get together to talk about life and plans. Rachel discovered that for years he had been seeing multiple different women. He was unrepentant and repeatedly accused *her* of causing his betrayals. My wife was able to be there to support her through the difficult time. Shortly after she and her husband separated, Rachel was diagnosed with cancer.

Rachel's husband made life difficult throughout the separation, her sickness and the divorce. He caused fights over money and the children. He spread lies about her illness and questioned whether or not it was even real. There were many times that she lay in bed helpless from the chemotherapy, needing the assistance of her brother, sister and mother for every part of survival. Her husband gave no emotional support or empathy during her many treatments and added stress to every engagement. After three years of battling her illness, Rachel died at the age of 36.

Betrayal is an intensely personal situation to endure and difficult to forgive. Betrayal is rampant in our society. More than fifty percent of marriages end in divorce. How many of those are ended due to infidelity? How many wedding vows are placed to the side with a ring on a motel nightstand? How painful is the discovery of the breaking of that trust? For wives and husbands the situation is devastating, but how much more difficult for the children of these broken homes? They do not understand the situation, but they feel the betrayal of a parent's unspoken promise to protect and nurture them. They are lost.

As a society, we are well aware of the betrayal that religious organizations have engaged in. The victims of the Catholic Church child-abuse scandal and resultant cover up is painful for the Christian church to face. The Evangelical Church is routinely beset by reports of a pastor falling to the temptations of an attractive church member or worse. Pastors and Priests are held to a very high standard and are quite often lifted up in the minds of church members to near deity.

When loyalty and desire come into conflict with the truth, my experience is that truth is what is left on the nightstand. The truth in these situations is rarely confessed freely. More often than not, the truth has to be exposed so blatantly that the culprit either has to admit it or appear insincere and dishonest.

I've already made a claim in this study that either Christianity is true or it is not and we have made a commitment to follow the evidence to where it leads. Christianity makes multiple truth claims that can either be verified or proved false. We have already successfully explored four claims of Christianity. Science, on the other hand makes no claims except that they cannot know the truth and that the best that they can do is to continue looking in spite of the impossible probabilities of finding the naturalistic causes for which they are searching.

Lawrence Krauss, atheist and theoretical physicist, explains when asked why the title of his book makes it seem as if the "questions about origins are over," he answers, "In the preface I tried to be really clear that you can keep asking "Why?" forever. At some level there might be ultimate questions that we can't answer, but if we can answer the "How?" questions, we should, because those are the questions that matter."[xxxv]

Reasonable people can accept uncertainties and different conclusions to an analysis of evidence. What would be considered a betrayal is for an authority to purposefully misrepresent evidence or interpret the evidence in a wildly dishonest way.

What if our government, our scientists or teachers were betraying our trust by presenting outdated and discredited evidence as a basis for teaching naturalistic theories? What if they presented these theories as fact in blatant disagreement with credible evidence? What if they held up known false ideas as intellectual necessities and convinced you to follow their lead? How would you feel?

Betrayed...

Exploring the Evolution of Life

Chance or Design

This is one of the biggies. Evolution versus creation! In our lesson on the creation of the Universe I said that we must be willing to look at all valid evidence and let it lead us to a reasonable conclusion. Are you willing to take this chance with me?

Christians are at a major disadvantage when we come to the Theory of Evolution because the theory is so well backed up by evidence that our society treats it as a fact. Is there any possible way that the scientists have gotten it wrong and that every school and every nature documentary has been duped into teaching a false theory? Our alternatives for how complex life came to be remain the same as they have been for the past few lessons. Chance is the champion of the scientist, while design is the choice of Christians. What does the evidence suggest is the most reasonable explanation for the existence of complex life?

Chance Advancements

The Theory of Evolution is the study of life forms to determine how they have developed their complexities and segregation. The evolutionist believes that by natural selection, the unguided chance of time and nature, life evolved in complexity from a one-celled lifeform to all of the different species that we see today. Random mutation (of DNA) and natural selection describe the concept of Survival of the Fittest. In an environment where a species lives, when there are challenges for survival, the ones that have genetic mutations that make them less susceptible to destructive forces will be the ones that survive and it is their DNA that gets passed down to the future. The idea of becoming stronger is associated with some chance adaption (mutation) of the DNA which provides an advantage for that part of the species. This section of the species then competes and survives better.

Darwin's Finches

School text books still use Darwin's finches as an example of such adaption. Through his research, Darwin noticed over the years that the size of the beaks of the finches changed. He reasoned that the DNA of the finches that were able to survive in drought conditions became the

dominant strain of the species. The other sect was unable to survive and
they died off.
Darwin said that this
was the beginning of
a new species of
bird.

However,
studies conducted
over the past 100
years show that beak
sizes of the finches
vary with the cycles
of drought and heavy rains. What was thought to be Macro-Evolution,
the evolution of a new species, was actually Micro-Evolution, the
adaption of the inherent finch DNA to foster survival in different
conditions. It was later noticed that finches which had developed on
different sides of a mountain range over the course of decades did not
mate with each other and so they were deemed to be different species.

It turned out that they were perfectly capable of mating with
each other, (one species) but that they simply preferred not to. It would
be comparable to a socialite from New York arriving in Australia.
Though the socialite and the aboriginal are perfectly capable of mating,
they would simply prefer not to. In the same way that the finches are
still 100% finches, the humans are still 100% humans and no new
advancement has been made towards a new species.

Micro-Evolution and Macro-Evolution

The difference between Micro-Evolution and Macro-Evolution is
significant. Micro-evolution (small-evolution) is accepted as a reality
by scientists, skeptics and Christians alike. Jack, one of my students,
said that he was certain that micro-evolution was real. When I asked
why, he stated, "Because if it did not, we'd all look the same."

Micro-evolution describes the adaptions of a species within
the parameters of its DNA. We see humans of all makes and models as
a result of micro-evolution.

Macro-Evolution, (big-evolution) is what is referred to by the
theory of evolution. Macro-evolution describes the change of one
species into another, presumably one more capable of survival. Species

are capable of producing offspring. Breeding between two different species is called hybridization. A hybrid offspring is incapable of forming offspring. Charles Darwin was puzzled by this problem and asked the question, "How can we account for species, when crossed, being sterile and producing sterile offspring, whereas, when varieties (*within a species*) are crossed, their fertility is unimpaired?"[xxxvi]

Fossil Record

Our minds usually go to the fossil record when we think of the evidence for evolution. We remember the graphic of a tree. At the foot of the tree is the common ancestor to all life. As you look up the tree, we see pictures of earlier species superimposed on branches and at the ends of the branches sit the various modern species. This is the Darwinian model of the theory of evolution that has  established itself as the sole scientific rail to explaining the complexity and diversity of life that we see today. The model seems to make sense and provides a powerful picture of how natural causes, not a creator, are responsible for life.

It seems to make sense that animals, including humans, came from less advanced, smaller versions of ourselves. In graphic form we see the common ancestor of monkeys and humans transforming into each branch in a matter of a few iterations.

We have the fossil record, taken from rock strata that date back to the formation of the earth and with each successive stratum layered on top of the other; life becomes larger and more complex. A young child could line up the smallest to largest fossils into a time-lapse graphic of how we came to be. This evidence seems very convincing, and unfortunately, this superficial evidence is as deep as most people Investigate. We have the benefit of looking deeper.

After more than 100 years exploring and investigating the evolutionary tree, scientists have uncovered at least two areas of evidence fatal to the theory of evolution: the Cambrian Explosion and DNA.

The Cambrian Explosion

The Cambrian Explosion describes the oldest strata of rock where "most major animal groups appear for the first time in the fossil record."[xxxvii] The layer of rock underneath the Cambrian layer is, go figure, the Pre-Cambrian strata. The Pre-Cambrian rock stratum has no fossilized remains except on the boundary between it and the Cambrian layer. Then, in the Cambrian layer there is an abundance of fully-formed, complex life. The problem for the evolutionist is that there are is no gradual formation of life as they expected. Life seemed to appear in an instant. Marine Biologist Paul K. Chien said, "What we are seeing is a quantum jump and this quantum jump has no explanation."[xxxviii]

Trilobites, which are abundant in the Cambrian stratum, have complex biological structures like a brain, gut, heart and compound eyes.

Richard Dawkins, an evolutionary biologist and leading voice of *new atheism* claims,

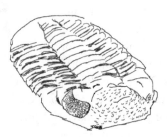

> *"Evolution ... must be gradual when it is being used to explain the coming into existence of complicated, apparently designed objects, like eyes. For if it is not gradual in these cases, it ceases to have any explanatory power at all. Without gradualness in these cases, we are back to miracle, which is simply a synonym for the total absence of explanation."*[xxxix]

Charles Darwin himself says,

> *"To suppose that the eye, with all its inimitable contrivances for adjusting the focus to different distances, for admitting different amounts of light, and for the correction of spherical and chromatic aberration, could have been formed by natural selection, seems, I freely confess, absurd in the highest possible degree."*[xl]

The fossil evidence of the Cambrian Explosion presents a graphic that evolutionists are having a difficult time reconciling with their theory. Their tree picture predicts that as they go backwards in time species will join together and become less complex. What they are seeing is that the branches representing diverse complexity actually extend all the way back to the beginning of the fossil record. There is no trunk, but rather lots of trunks that are independent of each other. The fossil evidence does not point to a common ancestor, but rather the sudden existence of *designed,* diverse life.

DNA

DNA is the code of life. DNA is a physical, chemical structure that contains information and which performs very precise work in accordance with its own instructions. DNA produces proteins which in turn do the work at the cellular level necessary to sustain life. The marvel of DNA is hard to overstate. "If all the DNA in one (1) of your cells were uncoiled, connected, and stretched out, it would be about 6 feet long. It would be so thin its details could not be seen, even under an electron microscope. If all this very densely coded information from one cell of one person were written in books, it would fill a library of about 4,000 books."[xli]

DNA poses a problem for proponents of evolution because there is no theory or understanding how information can be produced by nature. There are no examples in nature where information organizes itself and conducts work. The existence of productive, durable and flexible information simply defies any known method of development except for the method by which it is produced now, by an intelligent mind. Paul Nelson, a Philosopher of Biology at Biola University put it this way, "Only Intelligence can visualize a complex end point and bring together everything that is needed to actualize that end point."[xlii]

While Darwin lived, science had not yet learned about DNA. Scientists believed that cells were the lowest building block of life and that they were simple structures. Once we gained the ability to look inside the cell we have discovered the incredible design and immense complexity.

The trilobite of the Cambrian explosion offers a small example of the extraordinary amount of information that was present with the earliest life. The trilobite had at least 40 specialized cell types, each containing DNA and multiple other independent functions necessary for survival and reproduction. The information needed for the design of the trilobite as a system was far in excess of the DNA alone.[xliii]

To add to the overwhelming difficulty of sustaining the theory of evolution, the information in the DNA cannot account for the body type of a being. The information for the body type is contained in the embryo itself, so no matter how many times DNA is altered or mutated, and no matter how useful those mutations might theoretically be, they cannot change a body type. And to reiterate an earlier point, the majority of body types (animal groups) we see today were present in the earliest fossils. The DNA may be decorating the inside of the house, but it can't determine how many stories, rooms or the number of cars that will fit into the garage. Those plans reside outside of the DNA and remain a mystery.

Evolutionists are discovering multiple, independent sets of evidence that destroy their theory.

Irreducible Complexity
The identification of irreducibly complex building blocks within living cells is another knife in the heart of the Theory of Evolution. Michael Behe defines a system as irreducibly complex if it consists of several interrelated parts for which removing even one part renders the system's basic function unrecoverable.[xliv]

With the discovery of DNA and the ability to examine the machinery of the cell, scientists were able to begin to test the Darwin-assigned standards to the theory of evolution. Darwin himself says, "If it could be demonstrated that any complex organ existed which could not possibly have been formed by numerous, successive, slight modifications, my theory would absolutely break down."[xlv] Darwin placed this burden at the organ level. The same logic holds at the chemical level.

The most popular example of irreducible complexity is the bacterial flagellum. The bacterial flagellum is a high-functioning motor. In fact, it is far more efficient and powerful than any man-made motor. Its propeller rotates up to 100,000 revolutions per minute (rpm) and can reverse direction within a quarter of a turn. Imagine driving your car at 70 mph on the highway (approximately 3,500 rpm) and suddenly moving the gear shift into reverse. If you survive the crash, you will need to replace the mangled metal of your car engine and transmission.

The flagellum consists of 40 specialized proteins, which if any of them are removed the engine would become inoperable. Thirty (30) of these parts are unique to the flagellum and do not exist in any other capacity in the bacterium.[xlvi] David DeRosier, PhD, Professor of Biology at Brandise University argues that, "This is a machine that looks like it was designed by a human, but that does not mean that it was designed, that is a product of intelligent design. Indeed, this has all of the earmarks of something that arose by evolution."[xlvii] He says that the flagellum shares many of the same proteins with the *syringe* that some bacteria had with which they infected cells with the bubonic plague. The logic goes that the syringe is missing many of the proteins of the flagellum, but it is still a functional system and therefore the flagellum is not irreducibly complex.

DeRosier inadvertently exposes the very vulnerabilities of the evolutionary theory. He presents another irreducibly complex system without explanation and does not answer the question as to how the syringe turns into a motor through productive systems by the addition of one protein at a time. The challenge is similar to trying to turn an ax into a chainsaw. Evolution says that with every additional piece added to the ax it has to serve some advantageous function.

Reasonable Conclusion

The assumption of society is that the theory of evolution is an established fact. In light of that condition, most people do not attempt to refute the *evidence*, they either accept it at face value or they reject it completely without explanation. Christians have the ability to refute the evidence and reject it with detailed explanations. While Christians can point to the evidence of intelligent design, atheists like Richard Dawkins must reject the evidence as he wrote, "Biology is the study of complicated things that give the appearance of having been designed for a purpose."[xlviii]

Betrayal was the theme of the introduction to this chapter. I believe that students and society have been betrayed by the authorities who insist on teaching you that evolution is a proven fact, when they know full well that there is no evidence to suggest that the *apparent* design is not actually a design made by a designer.

Implications of Each Conclusion

Believing that life evolved from one simple lifeform to ever increasing complexity and diversity through natural selection is to claim that information has the ability to spontaneously create itself and that something that looks specifically designed was actually the byproduct of time and material. You are accepting that you are an unintended accident without value and with no real purpose.

Believing that life was the result of the will of God creates an obligation to seek the purpose of God's act of creating life. You are saying that God created your life and that he did not do it by accident. A reasonable person would seek to find the definite purpose in life if they believed that God created them. Ignorance of God's purpose cannot be an excuse for living apart from God when he has also provided insight through his written testimony we call The Bible.

> Answer the Assessment questions from the
> beginning of the chapter again

Characteristics of the Life Giver
- Powerful
- Personal
- Purposeful

Deliverables
- Atheist Evolutionary Biologists generally accept the appearance of design in life.
- The Fossil record shows that complex and diverse life appeared very quickly and without sufficient time required by the theory of Evolution. Cambrian Explosion.
- Information is only created by an intelligent mind. DNA is filled with specific, purposeful information.
- There is another level of DNA that determines animal forms. This level of information cannot be accounted for in the mechanism described in the theory of evolution.
- The theory of evolution fails when it is proven that large leaps of genetic information is required from one level of development to another. Irreducible complexity.

CHAPTER 6

Morals

Do Transcendent Objective Moral Standards Really Exist?

Possible Conclusions

1. No. Transcendent (Applying to All) Objective Morals do not exist. Truth is relative and though we may have a sense of right and wrong, good and evil, they are not grounded in anything besides our own preferences. The highest good is to increase human happiness and enhance human flourishing.

2. Yes. Transcendent Objective Morals do exist. The creator of the Universe and Life has also filled each of us with a moral sense that knows right from wrong, good from evil. The Transcendent Objective Moral Standard is part of the nature of God.

Assessment

Question	Before Reading	After Reading
Are you a good person?	Y/T - N/F	Y/T - N/F
Your moral standards come from your instincts.	Y/T - N/F	Y/T - N/F
Can Atheists be moral?	Y/T - N/F	Y/T - N/F
It is always better to pay for an item rather than steal it.	Y/T - N/F	Y/T - N/F
The Bible has a list of all things to do or not do.	Y/T - N/F	Y/T - N/F
Torturing a baby for fun is always wrong.	Y/T - N/F	Y/T - N/F

Morals Introduction

Was my positive self-image a farce built on delusion and the false evidence of success? The question of whether or not I was really a good person was one that I could not rationalize away and it would not disappear into the background as my life progressed. I had just destroyed my marriage and crushed any faith that my wife had in me.

I was agnostic with regard God throughout my youth and into early adulthood. My sense of *something more* was good for interesting conversations with my brother from time to time, but not really enough to push me to search for God. I was successful in high school without much effort and my time at West Point was transformative from a self-reliance standpoint because I had to work hard to succeed academically on my own. Along with the tough academics came the very strict honor code with which I never struggled. In the summer of 1991, by all appearances, I was a successful  young officer with a promising Army career ahead of me. But on a fateful day as I arrived home from work, my wife stomped out of the house as I walked up on the sidewalk.

She was shaking an open envelope in her hand and carrying her wedding ring in the other. I can't recall what she was yelling because the reality of what she had discovered drained me of every stable connection I had in my brain. In an instant I was numb. The envelope held a note from a young lady from out of town that I was attempting to meet with.

She turned and threw her ring.

Was I really a good person? I asked the question of myself knowing the answer. I was clearly a person willing to risk the love of my young wife for hidden selfish desires. I had no foundation for my moral actions except as they suited my career and kept up the impression of faithfulness with my wife. I could adjust my standards of good and bad with whatever situation I happened to be in. I could rationalize that things in my marriage were not good and that I was unhappy. Since my moral code revolved around my happiness, it was enough reason to cheat. But I knew what it meant. I knew in that moment that I was a broken person, far beyond redemption on my own merits despite how many good deeds I did. I was not a good person and I had to find out how to be one.

I was fortunate to have my human condition revealed to me in a very real way at a relatively young age. I was cleaver and smart and energetic, but I was also deceitful. My deceitfulness cost me my marriage and hurt a lot of people. I accepted full responsibility for my actions and I began to seek the truth of what it meant to be good.

What I learned was that I could not truly be good while clinging to my own standards. Praise from myself was worthless. I could not trust my own judgement of myself so how could I know if I was truly good? Think of the person who would praise you no matter what you did even when you knew you were not praiseworthy, "Oh honey, what a beautiful scratch on the car!" That praise is worthless because you know it's not true. Our personal standards of our own goodness change with our emotions and situations.

Through my search, I learned that there was a true standard for good and though I knew I could never be perfect, I did not need to be. When I found the true standard for good, I wanted to live up to that standard regardless of my current situation and in spite of my human cravings resisting that standard. I was able to trust the source that was judging me because it never changed. Not only was it constant, it was patient, merciful and forgiving.

Exploring Morals

The Moral Atheist

It is important to start this chapter with a major announcement so we can move on to the core of the contentions surrounding objective moral standards. NON-CHRISTIANS CAN ACT MORALLY AND MOST DO. CHRISTIANS CAN ACT IMMORALLY AND OFTEN DO. None of us are perfect. Paradoxically, this statement, which I believe would be accepted by any reasonable person, sets the stage for the core question of this chapter.

What are morals and where to they come from?

This lesson will examine the possible sources of morals based on the two worldviews that we have explored up to this point. Can a universal moral code develop through the chance creation of the Universe and life or is our moral sense derived from a creator?

The Moral Sense Exists

Yes. I am assuming that everyone has a moral sense. Anyone who truly does not is probably already in jail. You see, if morals did not exist, then the question of whether or not any of us were moral beings would not matter. If being a moral person was not important to our own conscience, then why would we care?

Even those who are prominent in the world of skeptics support the existence of moral standards from a source beyond humans.

Christopher Hitchens writes, "Human decency is not derived from religion. It precedes it." [xlix]

Richard Dawkins explains that, "It is a strong urge which exists independently of its ultimate rationale. I am suggesting that the same is true of the urge to kindness – to altruism, to generosity, to empathy, to pity". [l]

The publisher's description of non-theist in Sam Harris' book, *The Moral Landscape, How Science can Determine Human Values* [li], says, "Because such answers exist, moral relativism is simply false—and

comes at increasing cost to humanity. And the
intrusions of religion into the sphere of human values
can be finally repelled."

The urge to act morally is inherent in humans and it is essential to all of
us to act in accordance with our consciences. Whereas the Christian can
point to God as the source of their moral sense, the skeptic must
attempt to root their sense in some other source. Skeptics cannot deny
the sense of right and wrong because at the least, it is the justification
for them to even care about promoting their own beliefs.

Taking a Stand

Each and every one of us will take a position on issues that are
important to us. There are many hot-button issues today that would
separate people clearly on one side of the issue or the other. Abortion is
either right or it's wrong. Homosexual acts are either a sin or they are
not. Child abuse is good or it's bad. Terrorism is either righteous or
evil. Recognizing that we each make many moral judgements
especially when something affects us personally, then the question
becomes to whom should those judgements apply and why.

If the moral sense is rooted in ourselves, then the moral
judgement applies to us alone. If the moral judgement is based in a
higher source, then the moral standard can apply to all people at all
times in all places. The first case is called subjective, where the
standards reside in the individual subject. The second case is objective,
where the standard is outside of the individual or act.

The diagram to the left is objective. The square around the
earth represents a universal moral standard. The diagram to the right is
subjective. The multitude of squares represent the individual moral
standards that exist if there is no universal moral standard.

One Moral Standard from a source to which we all are subject that applies at all times to everyone, everywhere. There is objective right and wrong, good and evil

No one is subject to a higher moral power. Each person carries their own moral standard and decides what they believe is right or wrong, good or evil. All moral judgements are logically incapable of claiming an act or belief is wrong or evil.

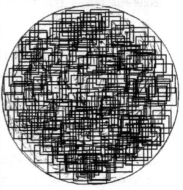

The Evolutionist's Moral Reach

It is perfectly logical to say that your moral sense was developed through the course of evolution and therefore is *not* a universal moral code. In this case, the moral judgements you make are rooted in your instinct or socialization and you cannot say for certain that someone else's moral code is not different or equally valid. Each person has their own, though probably similar, moral compass, but in the end we must admit that what is right for someone else is right for them and what is right for you is right for you.

It would not be logical to claim that a moral sense developed through the course of evolution was rooted in some universal code that applied to everyone. Evolution could very well have progressed differently and produced a different moral code. After all, even if a clearly defined code was identified, to what power would an evolved being be responsible?

Recognizing that each of us define good and bad, right and wrong differently allows us to be tolerant of other views and actions. What seems to be the only thing we can't be tolerant of, the only thing that is absolutely wrong, is when we are forced to comply with someone else's morality.

Absolute Moral Values

If we break that down a bit, what we see is that by making an absolute moral judgement about the injustice of being forced to live under someone else's moral code with which they disagree, the evolutionist is invoking a universal moral code for which they do not have a basis. (You may need to read that again – I had to.)

Going back to some of the hot-button items, is it absolutely wrong to deny a woman the right to abort her child? Is it absolutely wrong to deny equal rights to homosexual couples? Is it absolutely wrong to stone a woman to death for speaking to a man other than her husband? Someone with an evolutionary world view can at the most say that they agree or disagree with these acts but not that any of them are absolutely right or wrong for the people subject to them.

Are there any real absolute moral standards? If you can avoid saying that there are, then the evolutionary worldview holds true. However, if you must admit to even one absolute standard, something that is morally right or wrong for every person in any place at any time, then it demands the search for the power from which the standards came and to which everyone is responsible.

- Was slavery absolutely wrong?
- Was the holocaust absolutely wrong?
- Is racism absolutely wrong?
- Is the genital mutilation of young girls absolutely wrong?
- Is child pornography absolutely wrong?
- Were the Crusades absolutely wrong?

- Was the destruction of the men, women and children of the Promised Land absolutely wrong?
- Is it absolutely wrong that drunk drivers kill thousands of people every year?
- Would it be absolutely wrong for you to be fired because of your religion or lack of religion?

If none of these are absolutely wrong, then the conditions they represent imposed on you and your family would not be wrong either. You might be able to see how the relativistic (no absolute right or wrong) mindset could lead to beliefs about power and right and wrong that could be used inappropriately. When the people in power have a moral sense that it is right to remove the rights of a group of people and kill or enslave them, does that make it right? What if it were Christians that were singled out? What if it were everyone but Christians? What if they knocked on your door?

The Moral Standard
If, however, you believe that any of these or any number of other acts is absolutely moral or immoral for every person anywhere and at any time, then you are establishing a standard. You are acknowledging a moral scale where acts can be categorized as good or evil, right or wrong. They can even be graded from best to worst. Actions themselves are not the scale; they are graded on the scale. The scale is something completely different than the acts themselves and in order for an act to be rightly judged, the scale must have been provided by or reflect an authority to which all beings are accountable.

From an evolutionary perspective, this universal scale does not exist. What exists in that case are many smaller scales which reside within the minds of each individual and which hold no power over any other person.

The Comparison Between Two Acts
As soon as one act is identified as always right or always wrong, or just effectively, when two acts are compared to each other as one always being better than another, this scale is proven. For example is it always better to pay for an item rather than steal it? Is it always worse to kill a

child rather than nurture it? As soon as the scale is proven, the standard giver is proven.

Development of the Moral Sense

The existence of a transcending moral standard is perfectly in line with the Christian worldview. The Christian has no problem admitting that some things are absolutely right or wrong, good or evil. This is not to say that the moral law is some perfectly straight-forward list.

The truth is that our interpretation of the moral law is inherently flawed due to our separation from God, and the law is filled with nuances and grey areas that can only sometimes be resolved through an understanding of the situation in which the events took place. To be clear, though the Bible provides some clear direction on moral behavior like the Ten Commandments, it does not provide a neat and tidy list of all of the dos and don'ts of life. The Bible does present values that are to be pursued, which in turn direct our behavior;

> Matthew 5:6-9 is a subsection of Jesus' Sermon on the Mount:
> *⁶ Blessed are those who hunger and thirst for righteousness, for they will be filled. ⁷ Blessed are the merciful, for they will be shown mercy. ⁸ Blessed are the pure in heart, for they will see God. ⁹ Blessed are the peacemakers, for they will be called children of God.*[lii]

We see the values of righteousness, mercy, pureness, and peacemaking highly valued.

> Galatians 5:22-23 describes the expected result of accepting Jesus as your savior:
> *But the fruit of the Spirit is love, joy, peace, forbearance, kindness, goodness, faithfulness, gentleness and self-control. Against such things is no law.*[liii]

> 1 Corinthians 13:4-8 is the well-known verse on Love:

> *[4] Love is patient, love is kind. It does not envy, it does not boast, it is not proud. [5] It does not dishonor others, it is not self-seeking, it is not easily angered, it keeps no record of wrongs. [6] Love does not delight in evil but rejoices with the truth. [7] It always protects, always trusts, always hopes, always perseveres. [8] Love never fails.[liv]*

This verse is illustrative because it describes love in both positive and negative terms. It shows what love is and what love is not. The values that Christians are supposed to exemplify are demonstrated, explained and described throughout the Bible. Since we believe that God is the author of the Bible and the standard of Good himself, we trust the Bible where we may not understand every purpose. When no Universal power is accepted, there is no reason to follow any standard but your own.

Can Morals Evolve?

William Lane Craig presents the atheist's challenge for establishing a source of their moral sense in the following way:

> *On atheism, what basis is there for affirming objective moral values? In particular, why think that human beings have objective moral worth? On the atheistic view human beings are just accidental byproducts of nature who have evolved relatively recently on an infinitesimal speck of dust called planet Earth — lost somewhere in a hostile and mindless universe — and are doomed to perish individually and collectively in a relatively short time. "[lv]*

If you still have a desire to hold onto the relativism necessary with an atheistic worldview, there must be some explanation as to how your moral sense came to be. At what point in the evolutionary chain of events did the sense appear? Is it simply a residual instinct for survival? How could acting in a way we consider moral today, such as kindness, generosity, and self-sacrifice be developed in an evolutionary system that rewards just the opposite? How, when survival of the fittest means ruthlessness and destruction of competitive forces could these values persist and advance to today? Richard Dawkins asks,

> *"Let us try to teach generosity and altruism, because we are born selfish. Let us understand what our own selfish genes are up to, because we may then at least have the chance to upset their designs, something that no other species has ever aspired to do."*[lvi]

Summary

If morals are simply a societal sense of right and wrong that has been bred into us, then we can accept them as preferences without any basis for objectively stating that something is absolutely right or wrong, good or bad. If, however, we want the ability to logically assert that some acts are absolutely right or wrong for any person anywhere at any time, then we must say that there is a source of moral standards to which all people are responsible.

Implications of Each Conclusion

Believing that objective transcendent moral standards do not exist, then you can say that you do not like something or that you disagree with something, but you cannot say that it is absolutely wrong. You cannot say that the holocaust, slavery or the destruction of the occupants of the Promised Land were wrong, but only that you do not like that they happened. The hot-button issues of today lose their importance when you cannot claim the absolute moral necessity of accepting the homosexual lifestyle, of denouncing the brutalization of women under Sharia law, or of the evil of warfare.

Believing that transcendent objective moral standards exist demands that you discover the source of those moral values and learn to live in accordance with those moral values. When a source greater than the moral values is revealed to be outside of the creation itself, then it ties in perfectly with the God who created and fine-tuned the Universe for life and then created life, including yours. You must find out why.

> Answer the Assessment questions from the
> beginning of the chapter again

Characteristics of the Moral Law Giver
- Perfect

Deliverables
- Everyone has a moral sense.
- Evolutionists can claim to apply their morals to themselves, but must allow that everyone has their own moral sense to which they respond. They cannot say that anything is absolutely right or wrong, good or bad.
- Once an act or is deemed to be right or wrong for all people at all places at all times (objective and transcending) then it must be based on some standard external to everyone and to which everyone is responsible.
- Once a set of acts are compared to each other and one deemed to be always better than the other for all people at all places and at all times, then the transcendent objective moral standard is necessary.
- Every Standard has a standard giver.

CHAPTER 7

Evil and Suffering

Do evil and suffering in the world disprove the existence of God?

Possible Conclusions

1. Yes. Evil and suffering in the world prove that God does not exist. No all-loving, all-powerful god would allow the overwhelming and needless evil and suffering in the world.
2. No. God has morally sufficient reasons for allowing evil and suffering to exist. The evil and suffering in this lifetime take up the tiniest amount of time in light of an eternity of joy with God.

Assessment

Question	Before Reading	After Reading
Can suffering have a purpose?	Y/T - N/F	Y/T - N/F
Does evil exist?	Y/T - N/F	Y/T - N/F
An all-loving God would not want evil.	Y/T - N/F	Y/T - N/F
An all-powerful God would stop evil.	Y/T - N/F	Y/T - N/F
Someone can force you to love them.	Y/T - N/F	Y/T - N/F
If God exists, do you want him to respect the decisions you make?	Y/T - N/F	Y/T - N/F

Evil and Suffering Introduction

My grandparents survived WWII, though not without incredible sacrifice. Both of their families were Jewish. My grandfather was from Greece and served in the Greek Army. He survived Auschwitz, but his wife, daughter, mother, father, brothers and sisters were killed in the ordeal. My grandmother's family fled Split, Dalmatia with the clothes on their backs and crossed the Adriatic Sea to Italy. It was in Italy that they met and began their post WWII life together.

The world we live in and the conditions we see are a result of an endless number of variables being acted on by the previous set of endless variables. The murder of my relatives in WWII was evil. My existence is a direct result of their deaths. Many of us have similar types of stories and I would venture to say that if we went back far enough every one of us has an ancestor that came into the family through some evil perpetrated against their predecessor. How many African-Americans are here because of the evil of slavery? How many Irish are here because of famine and hardship? How many Chinese are here because of forced labor? Yet, today, even when there is unrest, we live in country dominated by peace and security.

My mother was nine years old when she and her family were set to come to the United States. As frustrating as it was, their departure from Naples, Italy was delayed by almost two weeks. There was a fair amount of stress during the delay and they could only think that by the time they set sail on the 31st of July, they would have already been in New York by five days if they had been allowed to travel on their original itinerary.

On July 31, 1956 they finally boarded the SS Constitution bound for New York. It's not clear if they knew that six days earlier, the ship that they were originally scheduled to take, the Andria Doria, had collided with the MS Stockholm and sunk.

"On C Deck, the worst loss of life occurred. A total of 26 people were killed in the collision section there, mostly Italian immigrant families."[lvii] I wonder how my grandparents felt when they learned the news.

Is it possible to know what God's plan is in these events and all of the ones that have happened before and after? I do not believe so. We can only observe our lives from our tiny perspective, tethered to the earth moving about in microscopic bits. Our brains, as amazing as they are, can only manage to keep a small number of variables in mind at one time and they suffer from ingrained selfishness that makes everything that happens to us somehow more dramatic and important that things that happen to others.

If there is no God, we are an accident upon an accident trillions of times over. If we are tortured to death or if we become highly celebrated is the result of yet more accidents and none of it is good or evil. If there is a God, then there can be good and evil and a purpose to both.

Exploring Evil and Suffering

Heart-Breaking Evil

The evil and suffering in the world is so overwhelming that it seems incompatible with a loving God. We turn our eyes from the television and listen with grief at reports of murders and genocides, of tsunamis and hurricanes. The loss of human life and the suffering that accompanies it seems to show a universe without a god. For what good god would allow tragedies such as the ones described below.

Notice: These are very disturbing accounts of real events.

Around the world;

> *"Harjare Kumenggar, said six Boko fighters surrounded her father, grabbed his dagger from his hands, slit his throat and sliced out his tongue in front of her. She was just 18 years old. She said they stole his motorcycle and kidnapped her two younger siblings."* [lviii]

> *Another "woman, Mariam Saidu, says she was kidnapped along with her six kids, put on a truck and kept in the encampment, where they were held captive in the Sambisa forest for nearly a year. She said they had to take husks of corn, grind it up and try to make a meal out of nothing. And some days, she said, there was nothing. She tells us with little emotion on her face that two of her six children withered away and died in that forest."* [lix]

And in our neighborhoods;

> *"Roberts had the 10 girls lie down facing the blackboard and he tied their hands and feet. Roberts told the girls he was sorry for what he was about to do, but "I am angry at God and I need to punish some Christian girls to get even with him. Roberts began shooting each of the girls before finally shooting himself. When the police broke in to the*

school, two of the girls, including Marian, were dead.
Naomi Rose died in the arms of a state trooper."[lx]

Unfortunately, I could fill many books with paragraph sized descriptions of heart-breaking examples of the suffering in this world. It is easy to understand why many people cry out, "Where God are you when these things are going on? Why would you allow this pain? Why not stop the evil?" People scream, plead and pray to God. People hate and reject God because of the world that they see.

Stephen Fry, an outspoken atheist, when asked what he would say to God if he one day met him responded, "I would say bone cancer in children? What's that about? How dare you! How dare you create a world in which there is such misery that is not our fault. It's not right. It is utterly, utterly evil."[lxi]

We will take this chapter to evaluate the thoughts that surround the existence of evil and suffering and determine if they are compatible with God or if they are evidence for the non-existence of God. Though we will not start with the presumption that God exists, it is instructive to see that the Bible does not shy away from the helplessness and frustration we feel when witnessing evil.

> *[2]How long, Lord, must I call for help, but you do not listen? Or cry out to you, "Violence!" but you do not save? [3] Why do you make me look at injustice? Why do you tolerate wrongdoing? Destruction and violence are before me; there is strife, and conflict abounds. [4] Therefore the law is paralyzed, and justice never prevails. The wicked hem in the righteous, so that justice is perverted.*
> - *Habakkuk 1:2-4*

All Loving and All Powerful?

Christians believe that God is all loving. 1 John 4:8 says, *"Whoever does not love does not know God, because God is love."* Certainly, if God is love, then he would want to stop the evil and suffering in the world. No loving God could watch what is going on in the world and not want to stop it. And Christians believe that God is all powerful. Jeremiah 32:17 says, *"Ah, Sovereign Lord, you have made the heavens and the earth by your great power and outstretched arm. Nothing is too hard for you."* Critics say that this is a logical contradiction in the character of God and therefore there is no God.

The critic claims that if God were all loving, he would want to stop evil and if he were all powerful, he could stop evil. Since evil exists, he is either not all loving or not all powerful, and that is not God. Certainly, in our personal experiences we see that where we have the power to do so, we keep others from doing wrong and we ourselves choose to do what is right. We are not gods, but the logic holds that the desire for good leads to decisions to do good and promote good amongst others. The Christian God is a conscious being capable of making choices for how he uses his power.

Free Will

If the statement above is true, then in it lies the seed for understanding the Christian God better and for understanding how God can exist while horrible evil and suffering occur all around. The statement also carries with it an insight that reflects who we are in relationship to God.

Genesis 1:26 says, *"Then God said, "Let us make mankind in our image, in our likeness."* We have free will to make choices. Our free will to choose is part of being created in the likeness of God. We have to acknowledge that we have responsibility for our free-will choices, whether we choose to do good or evil. The justice systems of the world are built on the personal responsibility that people have for the choices they make. The justice systems exist because people choose to do evil and cause suffering. So the question then becomes, can God control a world full of free-willed people? Can God control your free will? Would you want God to control you like a puppet master?

Free will is also central to the expression of love. Is it possible to force someone to love you? Think of someone that you love. Did that person force you to love them? Could they have forced you to love them? What about someone that has authority over you at work or school. What if they attempted to force you to emotionally love them? What would you think of that person? The ability to love requires free will. We realize that if people were forced to exist with no free will, then the controlling power would be considered unjust, ruthless and evil.

The closest example of forced will that we have here on earth is North Korea. CNN reported on a visit to North Korea that they had taken prior to the communist country's 70th Anniversary celebration, "As we drive around the North Korean capital, everywhere we look we see people carrying artificial red and pink flowers. 'Our joy is simply boundless! We're so overwhelmed,' says 18-year-old Sun Un Gyong." [lxii] Amnesty International reported, "Opposition of any kind is not tolerated. ...any person who expresses an opinion contrary to the position of the ruling Korean Workers' Party faces severe punishment and so do their families in many cases. ... Summary executions and long sentences of hard labor are still enforced."[lxiii] It seems that if a North Korean does not express boundless joy they could be incarcerated and tortured. Is it true joy if it is forced?

It is completely logical that an all loving God would want his creation to have the capacity for love. In order for love to be possible, free will is necessary. The consequence of free will is that though people can choose to love, they can also choose to do evil and cause suffering. Assuming we have all done something wrong before, how would we have reacted if God stopped us? What if God forced all of us into church on Sunday? God cannot control free-willed individuals and in the same way, we as free-willed individuals demand that God respect our decisions.

God is all loving and allows us to love through free will. Free will, by definition, means that it is not God's imposed will, and therefore God cannot control what we do. God's power is capable of doing everything that power can accomplish, which does not include controlling you or anyone else.

The evil we see in this world is caused by humans, not God.

Perspective

If you can accept that God can coexist with suffering then your relationship to suffering will be different. One perspective is to say that God does not exist and accept that our earth is a chaotic, meaningless and selfish place that just happens to grind people in the gears in a horrible fashion as a side effect of natural forces and evolution. The other perspective is to acknowledge that the existence of evil and suffering is not inconsistent with God's existence.

In the case where you have chosen to believe that there is no God, you are being consistent with the naturalistic, chance view of the creation and fine tuning of the Universe and the evolution of life. This choice also removes any basis for saying that something is evil. In the chapter on the existence of morals, we walked through the relativistic worldview necessitated by a denial of God. Without God, there is no source for transcendent objective moral standards. In the case of the existence of evil, you may be able to say that you do not like that girls are kidnapped and forced into the sex trade, but you can't say that it is evil. You would not do it yourself and you would prefer if people did not treat others that way, but what's right for you is right for you and what's right for them is right for them.

Let me put it another way, if no act is evil for all people at all places and at all times, then evil does not exist. If evil does not exist, then there is no basis for even discussing the co-existence of God with evil. If, however, some universal standard for evil exists, then it is rooted in a power greater than the individual and the Universe, and therefore God exists.

In our previous lessons, I tried to make it clear that if you accept that God exists, then you have certain obligations to seeking God's purpose for you. If God created the Universe and life for a purpose then what is that purpose? And if we can accept that God has a reason for creating us, then there would also be a purpose to the suffering that comes with every life.

> *⁶ In all this you greatly rejoice, though now for a little while you may have had to suffer grief in all kinds of trials. ⁷ These have come so that the proven genuineness of your faith—of greater worth than gold, which perishes even though refined by fire— may result in praise, glory and honor when Jesus Christ is revealed.*
> *– 1 Peter 1:6-7*

One insight we can see is by looking at one other trait that Christians attribute to God; that he is all knowing. In a world of free-willed individuals there is going to be evil. Perhaps God, who knows the end from the beginning, has arranged things so that the world has the greatest amount of good and the least amount of evil possible. God has arranged things for those who believe in him so that they can benefit from their struggles.

Value System

When you believe in God, and when you are able to spend time in the Bible and among believers, you realize that God does not have the same value system that the non-Christian world has. God does not hold your personal happiness as the highest value the way the world does. God is much more concerned about your holiness than your happiness. God desires a relationship with you and he desires your love, but he can't force it from you. Nearly without fail, those of faith who suffer difficult times are brought closer to God through the struggle. They learn to rely on him and to have peace through the process. They learn to trust the outcome to him. It is one of the defining characteristics of Christians that they are able to endure difficult times with a smile on their face and genuine peace in their hearts.

Ask a Christian about a struggle that they have had and what they learned about God through it. Then ask if they would replace that experience.

It is possible that God has a morally sufficient reason for allowing evil into the world. The possibility of love seems to be evidence enough. Bringing people closer to himself is reason enough. Allowing people to have hope in the face of difficulty is reason enough. The difference in perspective makes all of the difference when seeing evil and suffering and when experiencing suffering. Those with God have hope, those who choose to experience these events without God do not have hope except for physical deliverance from the suffering. For those without God, this life is all that there is. They have a certain number of years before their time of consciousness ends. Those who reasonably choose to believe in God have hope for eternity. 1 Peter 3:15 tells us, *"Always be prepared to give an answer to everyone who asks you to give the reason for the hope that you have. But do this with gentleness and respect,"*

The evidences provided in the previous chapters provide a set of characteristics about what we can know about the creator if he exists. He is eternal, powerful, and purposeful. We know from scripture that *"it is commendable if someone bears up under the pain of unjust suffering because they are conscious of God."* - 1 Peter 2:19 and from Revelation 21:3-4 *"³ And I heard a loud voice from the throne saying, 'Look! God's dwelling place is now among the people, and he will dwell with them. They will be his people, and God himself will be with them and be their God. ⁴ 'He will wipe every tear from their eyes. There will be no more death' or mourning or crying or pain, for the old order of things has passed away."*

The hope of Christians may be a mystery to those who have chosen to not believe in God. However, lack of understanding does not change the truth. Frustration at the *arrogance* of Christians for claiming to know the truth does not change the evidence. The hope of Christians is more than reasonable.

Respecting Free Will
Finally, understand that as you make free-will choices in life, God will respect those choices. If there is an eternity, you will make your choice here on earth regarding what Christian's claim is the only way to Heaven – Jesus Christ. If you choose to accept his sacrifice for your sins, then Scripture says you will be saved. If you choose to deny God and in turn, Christ, then Scripture says you will experience the alternative for eternity.

This is a weird concept for many people, but I encourage you to follow the logic, if not the understanding just yet. When Stephen Fry was asked if he thinks he would get into heaven states, "No. But I would not want to. I would not want to get in under his terms. They're wrong."[lxiv] It would seem to me that if you discover, after your death that God does exist and he's giving you a chance to enter Heaven, that all debate as to the rights of this all-powerful being to do as he pleases is over. I think I would jump at the chance to be forgiven even if I did not understand.

Implications of Each Conclusion

Believing that Evil and Suffering in the world prove that God does not exist is contradictory. If there is no God, then there is no such thing as good or evil. By choosing to believe there is no God also removes your ability to logically complain about evil or celebrate good. Good acts and evil acts become simply personal preferences. Each individual has their own preferences and governments have the power to implement whatever sets of values they prefer. This belief provides no basis for hope.

Believing that God exists along with evil demands that there is some purpose to the evil and suffering. God created a world where suffering and evil were possible for a reason. This belief provides hope through suffering and hope for eternity where there will be no suffering.

Answer the Assessment questions from the
beginning of the chapter again

Characteristics of the Free Will Giver
- All Loving
- All Knowing

Deliverables
- Evil exists
- Free-will exists because without free-will there is no capacity for love.
- Individual free-will, by definition, means God has given up the power to alter it.
- God offers hope for eternity no matter the suffering we experience during our life.
- God values holiness over happiness

- If someone rejects God, then they reject any basis for objective moral standards, and therefore evil is only a subjective judgement. A naturalistic worldview does not have a basis for good or evil.
- God will respect people's free-will decision with respect to Jesus Christ. If they choose to deny him, they will not be saved.

CHAPTER 8

Scripture

Is the Bible reliable?

Possible Conclusions

1. No. What Christians call scripture is not reliable. Their scripture has been compiled by men motivated by their own agendas and even if they wrote what they saw, their writings have then been modified and altered countless times over two thousand years. I cannot believe what is in the Bible.

2. Yes. Scripture is God's breathed word. It is his communication with the world to provide us with his plan for redemption. It was supernaturally inspired, written by men and has been supernaturally protected throughout its existence so that the words we read today are the words written by the actual authors.

Assessment

Question	Before Reading	After Reading
The New Testament has changed dramatically over time.	Y/T - N/F	Y/T - N/F
The disciples became wealthy as the leaders of the early church.	Y/T - N/F	Y/T - N/F
The New Testament is written in a way that could embarrass the disciples and Jesus.	Y/T - N/F	Y/T - N/F
The New Testament was written during the lifetimes of the disciples.	Y/T - N/F	Y/T - N/F
It was not uncommon for a disciple to	Y/T - N/F	Y/T - N/F

change his story in order to save his own life.		
There are thousands of early manuscripts of the New Testament.	Y/T - N/F	Y/T - N/F

Scripture Introduction

"It simply is what it is," my instructor told me. I sat in class contemplating how to accept her words because exceptions to the rule were so uncommon in the Russian Language. I was at the Defense Language Institute in Monterey, California studying the Russian Language for a year. We were in class seven hours a day and studied for several more hours in the evenings. Russian is one of the most difficult languages for English speakers to learn because of the different alphabet and sentence construction, and because every word seemed to be 23 letters long. We were learning the language as quickly as our brains could handle it.

Russian, however, is also a very structured language, which made it nice to learn. The rules are the rules. Russian is like the West Point parade of languages. Formations of cadets lined up perfectly, row after row exactly as you would expect – no surprises. If you learn the grammar rules you can apply them across the board with full confidence that you will be correct. It's not English, which has as many exceptions as rules. "Why is it geese instead of geeses?"

As we sat in class, our instructor was explaining to us one of the rare exceptions and we were having a hard time accepting it. We pushed hard to understand why such a structured language would allow such an obvious fault. "It simply is what it is. You must accept it," she insisted. Our instructor was a Russian native about 70 years old. She was fantastically smart and had grown up under communist rule so there could be an edge to her attitude as well. I realized that I was going to have to simply trust her because I had confidence that she absolutely knew the truth.

This kind of trust is different than trusting that an airplane is going to take off even though I can't explain why. It is different than a trust fall, where you close your eyes and fall backward trusting that your friend will catch you. This was an intellectual trust. I had to let go of what the rules said in order to accept the reality of what actually was. It was not easy and the episode left an impression.

The Scriptures face us with the same type of test for our intellectual trust. Are the Scriptures accurate? Have they been handed down to us reliably? Why should we believe what is written in them?

Exploring Scripture

What should we make of the book we call the Bible? Why should we
believe the things
written in it?
Scripture directs
the lives of 2.4
billion people
around the world,
so if it is inaccurate
or deceptive, those
people are living
according to a lie.

Scripture is like your refrigerator. If it is reliable everything tastes
good, if it's not things get smelly pretty quickly. Is everyone who reads
and lives by Scripture eating rotten food? Many people think that is
exactly what is going on. They believe Christians are eating rotten food
and passing it around to others as if it were filet mignon and the whole
lot of them are getting sick.

The reliability of the Bible is the most important issue of this
book. The Bible IS the Christian worldview. If Scripture is not reliable,
then everything that we claim about Christianity comes into question. If
it can be shown the authors changed the meaning of the Bible by
modifying passages, adding or deleting parts, then how can we know
what was originally written? If it can be shown that the Bible was
written by people who were not eye witnesses and that it was written
long after eye witnesses had passed away, then it may not be accurate.

Christians have everything at stake here, but so do non-
Christians. If the evidence shows that it is reasonable to believe that the
Scriptures are both true and accurate, then many other life-impacting
subjects become open for discussion. If Scriptures are true, then we can
arm wrestle about the existence of Hell, miracles the resurrection and
salvation. If the Scriptures are not true, then who cares about the rest?

Authors

Who wrote the New Testament scriptures that we have today? There
are plenty of reasons to scratch our heads and question the claim that
the rag-tag group of Jesus' followers authored the gospels and many of

the other books of the Bible. We are justified in asking about the agendas of the authors of the books of the Bible. What would they gain from creating the story of Jesus as Savior? Furthermore, how did their words get transferred to our current copies of the Bible? After playing a game of telephone with 30 middle-schoolers and seeing how a simple message can get completely changed as it gets whispered from one person to the next in less than two minutes, why should we believe that the method of copying the Bible was perfectly accurate over 2,000 years? Today's Bible may be completely different than what was originally written.

> New Testament scholar, Bart D. Ehrman, claims that many of the *"books in the Bible's New Testament were not passed down by Jesus's disciples, but were instead forged by other hands."*[lxv] He asks, *"So, if many of the books in the Bible were not in fact written by Jesus' inner circle – but by writers living decades later, with differing agendas in rival communities – what does that do to the authority of Scripture?"*[lxvi]

The obstacles to belief in what Christians call the Word of God seems to be too high to overcome, yet we must overcome them if Christianity is to remain a reasonable belief. If in addition to reasonable, I suggest that the Bible become the primary guide to your life, then what evidence is there to support your belief in it?

We will explore the following conclusions in the remainder of this chapter:

- The New Testament has been established to about 99% accurate. There are about 138,000 Greek words in the New Testament. Of these, only about 1,400 are uncertain today and affect no doctrinal issue.[lxvii] *(NOTE: Bart Ehrman agrees with this.)*
- The books of the Bible were written by eye witnesses a relatively short time after Jesus Resurrection[lxviii] (25-65 years after Jesus' death)
- We have over 5,700 early Greek manuscripts and another 9,000 in other languages.[lxix]

- We have complete New testament books from about 200 AD[lxx] (167 years after Jesus' death)
- We have the complete NT from about 250 AD[lxxi] (220 years after Jesus' death)

If all of this is true, why are scholars like Bart D. Ehrman so vocal about trying to disprove the Scripture? Unknown personal motivations aside, Dr. Ehrman rests his credibility on the inability to prove the inerrancy of the Bible. Dr. Ehrman says that any uncertainty of the New Testament text proves that it is not inerrant and uses that to justify making extreme claims about the corruption of the Bible. Dr. William Lane Craig, perhaps the most respected Christian Apologist working today, exclaims, "Good Bart knows that the text of the New Testament is virtually certain. Bad Bart deliberately misrepresents the situation to lay audiences to make them think that the New Testament is incredibly corrupted and uncertain."[lxxii]

A popular mouth rinse claims to "kill 99% of bad breath germs."[lxxiii] What would you think of someone who knew that to be true, yet spent their time vehemently arguing that it was completely unreliable? What if someone scored 99% on a difficult final exam and tried to complain to you that they did not know anything about the subject. Would that complaint be credible?

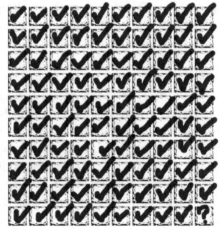

> *Bart Ehrman himself in his book, Misquoting Jesus, admits, "the essential Christian beliefs are not affected by textual variants in the manuscript tradition of the New Testament."[lxxiv]*

New Testament scholars have been able to take the manuscripts that we have and confirm that the Bible we are reading today is 99% accurate to what was originally written on those manuscripts. There is still the question of what kind of alterations were made between the time that the authors first put pen to paper and the earliest copies that we have of those works 70 – 220 years after the events.

Always Sacred

The evidence supporting the highly accurate maintenance of the original text is very strong. The history of the events witnessed by the authors was ALWAYS considered sacred and not subject to modification based on personal agendas. The life, death and resurrection of Jesus were highly disruptive to every disciple's life and far from what they expected. If they were to write a history that made sense to themselves, they would have stopped before they began. The real story was so far from what made sense to them that they could only write what they had witnessed.

Imagine that you are caught in the middle of your favorite end-of-the-world movie. Everything is crashing down around you and through a strange twist in the plot, you are at the White House where the President is motioning for you to come to him. You quickly low crawl across the debris to behind his desk where he is hiding. Explosions send flames and glass flying over your head. He pulls a set of papers from his breast pocket and shoves them into your hand exclaiming, "I have to keep the originals, but you must copy these plans exactly and get them to the Pentagon by sundown or all is lost!" You courageously take the plans and crawl further to the closet where you reach up and tear one of the President's clean shirts off of a hanger and start to copy the plans onto it.

The plan had some recognizable formulas and symbols, but several parts were strange physics symbols and things that you never even imagined in College math. "αδφ+_+=458444 4,99αωε δδδγασδι/33349108δκνϖ≅34()..." the plans went on for more than a paragraph and had some graphics that looked like a mix between an elephant and a flying saucer. "Exactly." You think. "Copy them exactly, the President said." And though you do not understand what it all means, there is no part you are willing to leave out because any piece could be critical to the people who know the big picture. You finish your work, toss the paper plans back to the President and dash out of the hole in the wall.

Just before sundown you drop through the ceiling of the Pentagon office where you meet the General who needs your plans. You unfurl the President's shirt on the table in front of him and a sense of relief overcomes you, until the door gets kicked in and dozens of people flow into the room. They start to lay pieces of curtain, chunks of drywall, and a mirror on the table. One guy pulls up his pant leg to reveal what everyone had copied; the exact same plan that you had.

The authors of the Scriptures knew that they were representing God in their writings and treated them that way. There was never a point where their goal was to write a self-help book for first-century people dealing with the stresses of the day. They were translating the very words of and plan of God in order to save the world. Following them, the scribes copying the original scriptures treated them as sacred. We have every reason to believe that the scriptures were transmitted precisely from the author to the earliest surviving copies.

Oral Tradition and Early Recording

The oral tradition of the Jewish society of the time was well versed at carrying on exact stories as they were originally presented. Considering that the disciples not only experienced the events, but then spent the remainder of their lives retelling the sacred events before writing them down, supports an accurate and true account of what they witnessed. Except for the books written by John (The Gospel of John, 1-3 John and Revelation) the books of the New Testament were completed 12 – 35 years after Jesus' death. The books by John were completed within approximately 60 years after Jesus' death.

The books were written by different men in different places at different times over the course of 50 years and yet they tell the same story in intricate detail. There are certainly areas that are difficult to understand and others that seem contradictory, but interestingly, those issues reinforce the authenticity of the text. The books of the Bible are exactly what you would expect if eye witnesses were writing under those conditions. If everything in the Bible matched without effort, then you might suspect that people gathered in a room to get their stories straight before putting out their final draft.

Authenticated in Blood

All of the disciples except John were put to death for their testimony about Jesus Christ. There are no records of any of the disciples recanting their story or confessing to a lie to save their life. They were killed in different ways by different authorities in different countries and they all died for the same reason. They proclaimed Jesus  as the Christ and their Lord and Savior. The stamp of authenticity to the truth of the New Testament books is marked with the blood of the eye witnesses. Many of us today would die for the Gospel of Christ, and though significant, it would not prove the truth of the Bible. Many people will die for things that they believe to be true, but no one will die for what they know is a lie. If the books, written by these men had contained lies, they would not have died for their content.

As we highlight their deaths, we can also highlight their lives as well as a testament to the truth of what they wrote. The disciples turned from their old lives and committed the rest of their lives to the building of the Christian Church. These men took a difficult path filled with danger, persecution and discomfort, while they could have chosen at any time to leave the church and rejoin normal life. None did. They did not gain wealth, power or women. They gave their lives for the teaching of the Gospel, which is exactly why there would be no tolerance for distortion or deception. To them, it was sacred and they were charged with passing on their sacred message accurately.

Had Peter rejected Christianity at some point and become a teacher debunking the lie of Christ, the society would have exalted him as uniquely credible. The Roman Government would have paraded him around as a celebrity instead of crucifying him. Paul's highly unlikely conversion to Christianity is another strong example of someone who had everything to lose and decided to purposely take the much more difficult path. He was a celebrity of the highest order in the Jewish faith. He was highly educated in Jewish Scripture and was a champion bounty hunter. He found and killed Christians for a living. Yet, he says that he had an encounter with Jesus Christ that changed the direction of his life. Though the event happened well after the crucifixion of Christ and his 'disappearance,' Paul was so moved that he not only stopped hunting Christians, he became one himself. He was then hunted and hounded for the rest of his life and yet he loudly proclaimed the gospel of Christ throughout the rest of his life until he was killed for his faith.

When we look to the motivations of those who have gone from Christianity to Apostate (rejecting Jesus) in spite of the evidence, what may motivate them?

Embarrassing

The disciples taught and wrote what they witnessed even if was embarrassing to them personally, and embarrassing to Jesus and the new religion. Peter denied Jesus three times while Jesus was being tortured. Peter, the *rock* of the new church placed revealing the truth of the events above the potential for personal ridicule. Why would he include such an embarrassing event if it was not true? They were all Jews with an expectation from Old Testament prophecy that their Messiah (Christ) would be a conquering king, not a humble servant. Who chooses to write a story where the hero dies unless it is actually what happened?

Intertwining of Old and New Testament

It seems as if there was a sense that the disciples did not know how the entire story fit together with the Old Testament Scripture, but they knew that it did somehow and they were prudent enough to maintain its integrity. Jesus references Old Testament prophecy to confirm his identity and the time.

16 He went to Nazareth, where he had been brought up, and on the Sabbath day he went into the synagogue, as was his custom. He stood up to read, 17 and the scroll of the prophet Isaiah was handed to him. Unrolling it, he found the place where it is written:
18 "The Spirit of the Lord is on me,   because he has anointed me   to proclaim good news to the poor. He has sent me to proclaim freedom for the prisoners   and recovery of sight for the blind, to set the oppressed free, 19   to proclaim the year of the Lord's favor."
20 Then he rolled up the scroll, gave it back to the attendant and sat down. The eyes of everyone in the synagogue were fastened on him. 21 He began by saying to them, "Today this scripture is fulfilled in your hearing."[lxxv]

The book of *Isaiah* was written about 700 years BC (Before Christ) and is part of the Old Testament. And better yet, it was recovered in its entirety, every word, as part of the Dead Sea Scrolls. One of the 20 copies of the book of *Isaiah* found in the Dead Sea Scrolls dates from approximately 125 BC.[lxxvi]

In many other verses, Jesus reaches back to Old Testament prophecies to reinforce their accuracy and clarify the future. The New Testament writers themselves then compound the intertwining of the Old and New Testaments by illustrating countless other prophecies and relaying new visions that correlate intricately with the ancient writings.

Massive Numbers of Copies
The high volume of copies that were made and the nearness to the original writings provide a great amount of confidence to New Testament scholars as to the accuracy of the texts. The number of early manuscripts is hundreds of times more than any other ancient writings. What we are seeing is that the eye witnesses wrote what they saw with great concern and that the texts were transported through the years with extraordinary care.

Early Church Fathers

The Early Church Fathers were students of the disciples and of the Apostle Paul. They were the disciples of the disciples and they continued the work of the eye witnesses. These men were a counterpart to the scribes in the sense that they took the scripture that they had access to and taught the church from those scriptures. These teachers were responsible for helping us close the gap between the original documents and the time that we have complete books of the Bible. In much the same way that pastors read from different parts of the bible now, the early church fathers' sermons captured parts of Scripture.

Twenty-five of the 27 books of the New Testament are cited by early church fathers by 110 AD, about 80 years after Jesus' death. The other two books are shown to be present well before this time through other indicators.

These second-generation teachers did not create Scripture. Not one of them is the author of any of the books of the New Testament. They were not eye witnesses!

J. Warner Wallace, a Cold-Case Detective and Christian Apologist puts it this way.

> *"If skeptics are looking for an early version of Jesus that is less divine, less miraculous and less supernatural, they are not going to find it in the writings of the first generation that followed the apostles. Instead, they're going to find the very same Jesus that you and I know from the writings of the New Testament."lxxvii*

Hey Dude

The early church fathers were ardent defenders of the books of the apostles and over the course of centuries, identified and eliminated non-authoritative teachings from amongst the Christian Church. Errant teachings and cults were harshly attacked as frauds as it was critical to protect the lay people from false teaching. *"There are some who trouble you and want to distort the gospel of Christ"* Paul writes in Galatians, *"8 But even if we or an angel from heaven should preach to you a gospel contrary to the one we preached to you, let him be accursed."* (ESV)

Beatles' fans would act the same way if someone claimed to have found a lost Beatle recording or released an edited version of *Hey Jude* titled *Hey Dude*. The fans would pull out millions of copies of the original and  refute the claim that it was *Dude* instead of *Jude*. The long-lost song would be compared to their other recordings, and a hunt for the recording studio and producer would be on. Fans would not stop until the origin of that song was verified. If it was verified, then they'd rejoice. If it was discredited, the song and the person promoting it would be vilified.

That's exactly what happened with second and third century claims that *new* Gospels had been found. The *Gospel of Thomas* is one such writing that claimed to be written by an eye witness, but which was rejected by overwhelming evidence as a fraud.

Implications of Each Conclusion

Believing that Scripture is not reliable frees you from taking what it says seriously. Even in the case where you take part of it and reject part of it, you have made a choice to conform Scripture to your personal preferences, which can change at any time. Though the Bible might have some good moral teaching in it, you are free to pursue your happiness in any way you see fit. Even if you maintain your claim of being a Christian, you have entered the world of relativism where each person is free to choose what they are going to believe. You have abandoned your ability to claim scriptural right from wrong.

Believing that Scripture is reliable obligates you to living according to its precepts. If God sent his word to the world and had people meticulously carry it through history to us today, then there is a purpose in his message to you. It gives you an amazing treasure of wisdom spoken to you directly from God.

Answer the Assessment questions from the
beginning of the chapter again

Characteristics of the Author of Scripture
- Eternal
- All Knowing
- All Caring
- Purposeful

Deliverables
- 30-33 AD Eye Witnesses walk with and learn from Jesus
- 45-95 AD Eye Witnesses teach and write separate books over 50 years
- 36-100 AD Eye Witnesses go to their deaths maintaining the truth of their books
- 33-100 AD Church Fathers learn from the eye witnesses
- 45-363 AD Church Fathers teach from the books written by the eye witnesses
- 45-363 AD Scribes copy the books thousands of times
- 363 AD Church Leaders meet to recognize the books as the inspired word of God and include them in one book, the Bible.
- The Bible we have today is established to 99% accuracy of the original books

CHAPTER 9

The Flood

Did the Biblical Flood Happen?

Possible Conclusions

1. No. The flood did not happen. The flood is a common myth, but it is impossible for a worldwide flood to happen.
2. Yes. The worldwide flood did happen.

Assessment

Question	Before Reading	After Reading
The Plate Tectonic Theory explains the features we see on the earth.	Y/T - N/F	Y/T - N/F
Fossils are produced in slow processes.	Y/T - N/F	Y/T - N/F
Rock strata do not extend over large areas.	Y/T - N/F	Y/T - N/F
The Plate Tectonic Theory does not predict the location of most volcanoes very well.	Y/T - N/F	Y/T - N/F
Rocks break, they do not bend.	Y/T - N/F	Y/T - N/F
The flood story is mainly a Judeo-Christian story.	Y/T - N/F	Y/T - N/F

The Flood Introduction

My middle son ran into the house and into my office. He was out of breath, "Dad! You need to come. Brace Fell out of the tree!"

My kids were 11, 8 and 7 at the time and we had been in Tennessee for a little over a year. It was our first summer in our new home. A creek ran through the property. Over the creek was a tree. The situation was perfect for an injury, it almost demanded it. Kids, warm weather, creek and tree.

I ran through the yard to the creek, where my oldest son was on his hands and knees in about 10 inches of water. I could see that his right leg at the ankle was bent at an unnatural angle. I knew that his leg was broken. I jumped into the creek and comforted him with my words as I lifted him like a calf as gently as I could. I kept telling him that it was going to be ok. I laid him on his back on the grass with his knees bent.

In the background, my mind was working on how to get him to the hospital. As I calmed him, his Grandfather returned home and was able to stand by him while I ran to the house to get my keys. I figured, with a broken leg I could put him in my vehicle and get him to the hospital faster than an ambulance could make it to my home in the country. I ran across the bridge over the creek and glanced back at my son laying there when I saw it. I saw something white on his shin.

"Where did that come from," I thought. Then I realized that I was looking at bone. I stopped in my tracks and told my father-in-law to call 9-1-1. There was no way I was going to try to move him in my vehicle with exposed bone. The shin on his non-broken leg was torn open for about five inches.

Today, if you look at his legs you can see the large scar and 16 stiches that he received on his shin. Now, when May rolls around and he's running around in shorts people ask, "What happened?" He tells the story of reaching too far out for a 'monkey ball' to throw at his grandfather's car as he drove down the driveway. He says that he broke his leg and had a large gash in his shin that was cut as he passed a branch on the way down. He tells how, by the grace of God, he landed perfectly between two large rocks and on his hands and knees instead of his head or his back.

Boys…men, are happy to tell others about how they got their scars. After we recover from whatever caused them, we are more than happy to tell people how we endured the trauma, the pain and agony and earned our badge of machoism. The earth, however, cannot tell us about its scars so we have to try to figure it out based on what we see.

Did you know that the earth has a long stretch of exposed bone called the mid-Atlantic trench? Did you realize that the earth has multiple unhealed fractures that do not correspond to the typical fault lines identified by the plate tectonic theory? Did you realized that hardened scar tissue covers most of the surface of the earth, and that all of the evidence points to the earth falling from the top of a giant tree and fracturing most of the bones it its body? The scars of the earth indicate that they happened in a very short time, a matter of months and within a few hundred years as opposed to the millions and billions of years proposed by most geologists.

Exploring the Flood

The Worldwide Flood depicted in the Old Testament of the Bible is hard to imagine. A worldwide natural disaster is unheard of in human history except for the Flood. Every other massive event we have ever read about or witnessed in modern history is extraordinarily small by comparison. The largest hurricanes, earthquakes and tsunamis are tiny in comparison. In 2004, an earthquake in the Indian Ocean caused a tsunami that devastated the shores of multiple countries killing over 230,000 people and injuring 500,000 more.[lxxviii] That event was like spilling a glass of water on yourself compared to what the Bible describes as Noah's Flood.

If the Flood theory is correct, there are several major questions that have to be answered. Where did all of that water come from, was it enough to cover the mountains of the earth, and where did it go? I will not cover the size of the Ark or the number of animals that could fit into it. There are plenty of great sources that have done the calculations to satisfy those questions. I will focus on much more tangible evidence to determine if the flood happened or not. Geological events leave scars on the earth's surface that can be evaluated as evidence and since we are evaluating the largest of those events, there should be large scars.

Earth's Scars

It is fair to say that the Earth is not a teenager any more. There are signs of wear and tear, wrinkles and aging. Does the earth show that localized trauma and generally uniform processes over the course of billions of years created what we see or is there evidence that a worldwide flood changed the face of everything about 4,500 years ago? There are three major pieces of evidence that must be explained by any theory of the Earth's current state.

1. How did the rock strata and fossils form?
2. How did volcanoes and fault lines come to exist?
3. How did major canyons form?

The best evidence I have seen to explain the geology of the earth from any source, is captured by Walt Brown, Ph.D, in his book, *In the Beginning, Compelling Evidence for Creation and the Flood.* Dr. Brown did not start at the Bible and try to make the geology match the story. He started at the geology to determine if it was reasonable to conclude that a worldwide flood had occurred.

Two Main Geological Theories
The first theory is involves billions of years and is called the Tectonic Plate Theory. The Tectonic Plate Theory is the accepted geological model taught in schools. It is accepted by the scientific community in general. Interestingly, the theory is only about 60 years old. According to this theory, earth's crust is "composed of many plates, each 30–60 miles thick. They move relative to each other, about an inch per year."[lxxix] The locations where the plates are moving in opposing directions meet, the earth experiences earthquakes and volcanic action. The theory contends that the evidence we see on earth, like mountains, continents and ocean trenches are the result of these movements and Geological processes over the course of millions of years. The tectonic plate theory and those that attempt to explain sedimentary layers and fossils incorporate "the principle of uniformitarianism, which states that all geological features can be explained by today's processes acting at present rates."[lxxx]

This theory is not generally contested, even by Creationists, since it is assumed that plate tectonics are the most evidentially supported theory, and except for the eons of time, it is not overtly contrary to God's Word. There are however, some major challenges to the theory. The theory cannot explain most of the major features of the Earth and cannot account for how a worldwide flood may have happened.

The alternative theory is the Hydroplate Theory. The Hydroplate Theory was developed by Walt Brown, Ph.D., when he started searching for the source of water that carried Noah's Ark to the heights of Mount Ararat. Though the search for the Ark goes on, the evidence he gathered for such a flood began to mount up. The Hydroplate Theory suggests that the earth's crust was originally sitting on top of an underground bed of water. (Figure 1)

Figure 1 (*54*) Crust sitting on Bed of Water

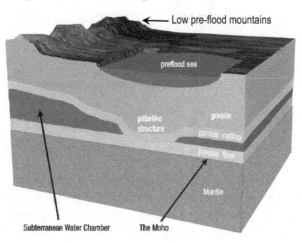

The crust, weakened with centuries of movement caused by the moving gravitational pull of the moon and finally burst on the Atlantic side of the earth. (Figure 2)

Figure 2 (*56*): Current day Atlantic side

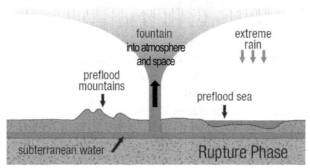

The initial rupture followed the path of least resistance around the earth and the powerful water rushed into the atmosphere taking massive amounts of soil and vegetation with it. The muddy water covered the earth sifted in to layers creating the rock strata and fossil record that we see today. (Figure 3)

Figure 3 (*58*) Extreme Rain and Sediment

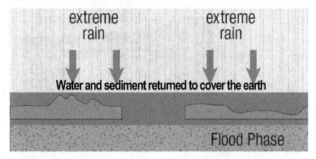

As the Atlantic side of the earth released pressure, the core of the earth moved that direction, pulling the crust under the Pacific Ocean inward creating weak points around the perimeter where earthquakes and volcanic activity takes place today. (Figure 4 and 5) The continents moved away from the Mid-Atlantic Ridge until the water they were riding on ran out. When they stopped moving there was a massive compression event that folded the still-soft strata into mountains.

As the water receded from the land, large volumes of water were captured in highland lakes. The lakes continued to fill and they eventually overflowed their banks, flooding through the layers of sediment, creating the Grand Canyon and others like it in a matter of days.

There are a lot of moving parts to this theory and summarizing it can be difficult. We will hit the big points, but a great video overview and the entire book is online for free here http://www.creationscience.com.

Figure 4 (*62*)

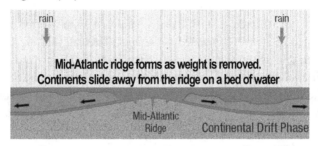

Figure 5 (*82B*)

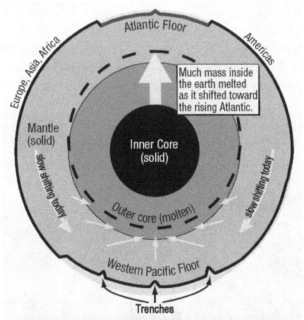

Rock Strata and Fossils

The layers of sedimentary rock covering most of the surface of the earth contain the fossil record. Both the strata of rock and the existence of fossils point to a very rapid, large-scale event involving massive amounts of water rather than a slow process.

"Earth's crust is frequently stratified with layered rock (or strata) composed of cemented sediments. These layers are typically parallel, thin, uniform in thickness, vast in area, and tipped at all angles within mountains and under valleys."[lxxxi] As you drive through cutouts on the highway, you can see the sedimentary rock strata. Geologists know that the material was initially loose like sand, and needed water, pressure and a cementing agent to turn them into rock.

Once cemented, the rock is hard. That is obvious, of course, but the hardness of sedimentary rock means one thing, it breaks, it does not bend. The rock strata that we see all around us is warped and molded in fantastic shapes without breaking. Mountains are formed from unbroken layers of rocks often folded on top of each other and surprisingly carrying fossils and shells of sea life on their uppermost surfaces. The sedimentary layers, often in the exact same order, cover continents and even straddle continents.

- There are no slow mechanisms like wind, rain, or rivers that can account for the massive, nearly uniform spreading out of these layers or for the pressure necessary to cement them.

- The evidence points to a rapid lying out of the sedimentary rock strata in water and that while the strata were still moldable, compressed into mountains.
- The slow pressures of the tectonic plate theory would mean that rock layers were formed and then lifted. It cannot explain how these layers were not broken during the folding. In fact, the theory cannot even explain how the force moved the rocks into mountains instead of crushing the rock at the point where the force was applied.

Layered Fossils

"Fossils rarely form today, because dead plants and animals decay before they are buried in enough sediment to preserve their shapes. We certainly do not observe fossils forming in layered strata that can be traced over thousands of square miles."[lxxxii] Fossils are formed when sedimentary materials rapidly kill and encase an animal. The material encasing the animal is then quickly cemented, preserving the animal's remains. The sedimentary rock layers around the world contain an abundance of fossilized remains, including soft bodied animals, those still eating and giving birth.[lxxxiii] Sea life and land animals are frequently jumbled together in the same area far from the sea.

1. Slow processes over the course of billions of years cannot account for the number of rapid disasters required around the world to create the fossil record. By definition, slow geological forces cannot account for rapid, massive fossil preservation. You cannot hit a homerun in slow motion.
2. Massive amounts of sediment rapidly covering the earth, capturing animals and plants of all types under enormous pressure, containing the cementing agents necessary to fossilize animals is consistent with the worldwide flood.

Fault Lines and Volcanoes

Fault lines are disruptions in the earth's crust. They are signs of trauma and they remain a weak point in the earth's crust where the pressures from shifting are released. If you have a ceramic pot that cracks down the middle in two pieces, it is possible to fit it back together and add some glue. The next year when you put soil into it and tamp it down with a little pressure, where will the pot break? The hard crust of the earth is like that.

The deep breaks in the earth's crust are mainly in the Pacific Ocean. The Pacific Ocean is outlined by 25,000 miles of fault lines called the Ring of Fire because of the accompanying volcanoes. "More than half of the world's active and dormant land volcanoes and 90% of the world's earthquakes occur along the Ring of Fire."[lxxxiv]

Figure 6 Ring of Fire

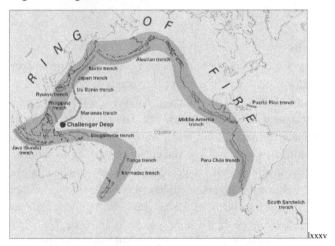

[lxxxv]

Figure 7 (*82B*)

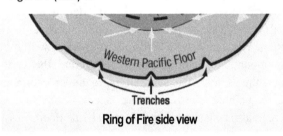

Trenches

Ring of Fire side view

The tectonic plate theory explains that the earth's trouble with earthquakes and volcanoes is the result of tectonic-plate bumper cars. It says that earthquakes occur where the plates bump into each other or slide against each other creating avenues for magma to reach the surface of the earth through volcanoes. However, the history of geological movement of the earth reveals major contradictions to the theory which make it questionable.

Two large US quakes were nowhere near plate boundaries. The "quite powerful, New Madrid, Missouri and Charleston, South Carolina earthquakes were" far from plate boundaries.[lxxxvi] In addition to those earthquakes many happen at depth far too deep to be explained by plate tectonics. "How can earthquakes occur 250–410 miles below the earth's surface where (a) pressures are so high that space cannot open up to allow movement, and (b) temperatures are so hot that rock does not break, but slowly and quietly deforms or flows?"[lxxxvii]

Finally, "Most volcanoes on the western Pacific floor lie on the wrong side of trenches," away from where the plate tectonic theory predicts that they should be. [lxxxviii]

The Hydroplate Theory contends that earthquakes and volcanoes are the result of the ongoing settling of the earth's crust and interior. The vast amount of the settling happened shortly after the flood event, but there is still some going on today exactly how and where you would predict if the type of rupture had happened. The claim that the earth is settling is important because it aligns with the evidence that when an earthquake happens, the earth becomes more compact and its rotation speeds up.[lxxxix] A research scientist at the Jet Propulsion Laboratory calculated that the 2011 Japanese earthquake should have sped up the earth's rotation by 1.8 microseconds, the 2010 Chile earthquake by 1.26 microseconds, and the 2004 Sumatra earthquake by 6.8 microseconds.[xc]

The key question is what is the earth settling from? If it's been formed for billions of years without major disruptions, then it would be at a point of equilibrium without the need for settling.

Plate Tectonic Fault Lines: Rock Bending and Not Breaking

The tectonic plate theory relies on the impossibility of rocks bending. If you recall, rock does not bend, it breaks. The theory suggests that 30 miles of gigantic slabs of rock actually bend between 30° - 60° and go under (subduct) another 30 mile thick slab of rock. Geologists cannot explain how the subduction began, they have no evidence of it occurring and physics does not support the theory. [xci]

If two 3-foot thick pieces of Styrofoam floating on water were pushed into each other without the ability to go up or down, they would disintegrate where they met. If, however one was able to go under/over the other, then it would follow the path of least resistance, which would be to move upward, not downward. Subduction does not explain the evidence we see.

A Giant Sinkhole Surrounded by Fault Lines

A casual look at the movement of the earth's crust shows that most of the movement is towards the Pacific Ocean. If the bumper car scenario of plate tectonics were true, then a much different picture would be expected. Plates would be moving in all different directions rather than acting like cows coming from all around the pasture to the barn for feeding time.

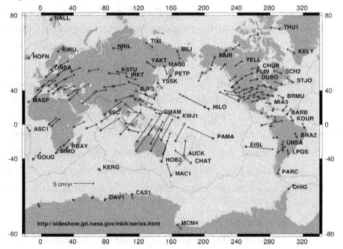

The crust movement is consistent with the Hydroplate theory because it suggests that the Atlantic Ocean side of the earth is where pressure was reduced as a result of the tearing away of earth and water from the rupture. With less pressure on that side, the core of the earth moved that direction, pulling the crust under the Pacific Ocean inward creating weak points where earthquakes and volcanic activity takes place today.[xcii]

The Formation of Canyons

As scars go, the Grand Canyon is a doosy. It, and others like it, are great evidence for the worldwide flood. To be fair, if the millions-of-years explanation that the Colorado River was responsible was viable, there may not be much of a controversy. However, "Though scientists have studied the canyon for more than 150 years, a definitive answer as to how or when the canyon formed eludes them."[xciii] There are several major reasons why the traditional explanation does not make sense starting with the missing material.

It's a joke in the Army that we sometimes work hard to dig a hole and then just as hard to fill it in. After digging the hole there is a corresponding pile of dirt on the ground next to it. That is not the case with the Grand Canyon. It's like looking over the rim of the hole and not seeing any pile of dirt. If the Colorado River dug out Grand Canyon, where did all of the dirt go? It is missing. "That question still bothers geologists, because if the Colorado River carved the canyon, as commonly assumed, there should be a gigantic river delta where the Colorado River enters the Gulf of California."[xciv] "About 800 cubic miles of material were removed in carving the Grand Canyon. The Colorado River's delta does not contain even 1% of this missing material. Where did it go?"[xcv]

Another major problem with the Colorado River theory is the existence of "dozens of large side canyons" connecting with the Grand Canyon that have no source of water.[xcvi] They do not match what would be expected if small rivers over time had eroded them. All of the evidence suggests that they were formed at the same time as the Grand Canyon. Furthermore, "a few side canyons are 'barbed.' That is, they connect to the main canyon 'backwards.' Tributaries almost always enter rivers at acute angles, but the barbed canyons are oriented at obtuse angles." [xcvii] If millions of years and rivers did not form the Grand Canyon, what did?

According to the Hydroplate Theory, as the flood waters drained off the continents they left behind post-flood lakes. Two large and growing lakes were atop the Colorado Plateau. The larger of the lakes breached its southwestern boundary, causing the smaller lake to also breach. The combined waters of both lakes spilled off the western edge of the Colorado Plateau and swept off the soft sediments south and west of the lakes carving the Grand Canyon in weeks.[xcviii] And the dirt is where you would expect it if a cataclysmic event had happened.

The Gulf of California is filled with the sediments from the Grand Canyon, but it was not neatly placed there by a river forming a nice delta, it was pushed there along with the rush of the water from the overflowing lakes. The sediments were pushed far into the Gulf where they settled and where we see them today.[xcix]

Reading the Scars

The purpose of this chapter is to encourage you to reevaluate your thoughts about the worldwide flood. Noah's Ark and the Biblical Flood are one of the most taught subjects of early Christian education. That is great because it makes for great story time, but it also poses a problem because by the time you are 10 you think you know everything you can possibly know about the Flood. To make matters worse, Hollywood, knowing that it makes for great drama and profit, produces a distorted movie about it. The fact is that the scars of the earth are the evidence for the worldwide flood.

Implications of Each Conclusion

Believing that a world-wide flood did not occur means that you accept the current theories surrounding the compilation of the earth and how the different parts work on each other. You accept the limitations of these theories to correctly explain the features we see today, predict what will happen next, explain how they happened, and what the results of those actions will be. You are also rejecting a significant portion of Scripture.

Believing that the world-wide flood did happen aligns your beliefs with Scripture. It should encourage you to compare the theories surrounding the cause and effects of the flood to determine if the Hydroplate Theory or the Plate Tectonic Theory is correct.

Answer the Assessment questions from the beginning of the chapter again

---

Characteristics of the Flood Producer
- All Powerful
- Purposeful

Deliverables

- The features of the earth we see today happened over a relatively short period of time, weeks and years, not billions of years.
- The sedimentary rock strata that cover the earth could only have been placed by a worldwide flood that happened very quickly.
- The plate tectonic theory acting on the earth over millions of years fails to explain the
  - Rock strata. No mechanism of wind, rain, rivers etc. can explain the consistent layers and organization of rock strata found around the world.
  - Fossils found in the rock strata. Fossils can only form when the animal is killed quickly, encased in sedimentary rock and put under pressure. Slow processes cannot do this and certainly not enough to leave world-wide evidence as we see.
  - Volcanoes and the locations of volcanoes. Wrong side of fault lines.
  - Earthquakes. Thirty-60 mile thick rock does not bend to subduct under another equally thick slab of rock.
  - Large canyons like the Grand Canyon. Every sign shows a rapid formation of the major canyons.
- The Hydroplate Theory explains the world-wide geological features we see today and properly predicts the effects of earthquakes and location of volcanoes.

CHAPTER 10

Hell

Does Hell Exist?

Possible Conclusions

1. No. Hell does not exist. Hell is part of the myth of a supernatural afterlife and is used to scare people into submission to religious doctrines.
2. Yes. Hell exists. Hell is an integral part of God's plan for justice. Hell is the eternal destination for people who remain responsible for their own sin as a result of not accepting God's mercy offered through the cleansing blood of his son Jesus.

Assessment

Question	Before Reading	After Reading
If something is legal does that make it moral?	Y/T - N/F	Y/T - N/F
There are multiple ways to Heaven.	Y/T - N/F	Y/T - N/F
If someone gets away with a crime are they innocent?	Y/T - N/F	Y/T - N/F
Should God send a good person to Hell?	Y/T - N/F	Y/T - N/F
Hell is where people are tortured for eternity.	Y/T - N/F	Y/T - N/F
I believe in justice.	Y/T - N/F	Y/T - N/F

Hell Introduction

The school bus was overfull and kids were standing in the isle. It is a situation that would not be allowed today but in 1977 it was not uncommon. I sat in my seat mad. I was not mad because of the kid standing too close to me in the isle, I was mad because of what I had just witnessed. To be honest, I was mad because I was so scared. I was new to the American School system in Furth, Germany. I was 12 years old and had not broken 100 pounds yet. I did not know anyone on the bus, but I was certain that what I had just heard was totally wrong.

I was scared and mad because I had just heard an older boy describe what would happen to him if he did not accept Jesus Christ as his savior. The older boy had short dark hair and he was standing looking down on the younger boy seated in front of me. He authoritatively described the torment in Hell and then he went on:

> *"Imagine that the Sun was a solid stainless-steel ball, and a dove flew from earth to the sun and ever so slightly brushed one of its wings against the surface of it and then flew back again to earth. If the dove kept making that trip, back and forth, back and forth, by the time that the stainless-steel ball had worn down to nothing – eternity has just begun."*

I was so mad I could spit, but not assertive enough to say something. I hated that this young man was putting that kind of fear into the boy in front of me. You do not convince people by scaring them.

In the moment I heard the story, my subconscious recognized the implications of what he was saying. I did not connect Jesus Christ to the equation yet, but I knew that his description of eternity was correct and I instinctively went into defensive mode because I had not met the standard to avoid Hell. "That is a cruel god who would torture people forever!" I thought, and I placed the blame on the kid who was presenting his view.

I was 12 years old and without a Christian foundation. I was wrestling with the version of reality I had just heard and which seemed very real. I was mad because the symbolism was so very vivid and the punchline was obviously true and troubling. In 40 years that event has never receded to the back of my mind, and I wonder where the two boys are today.

Eternity is something that we all have to wrestle with and though many will claim that there is no such thing, it can't be comforting to face convincing evidence that it is in fact real. I do not believe that fear is the best reason to choose Christianity, but it's better than nothing if it gets you moving in the right direction.

Exploring Hell

The existence and nature of Hell is highly disturbing to many people, including Christians. Why would God send people, even good people, to a place of torment for eternity?

Hell is an important component of Christian Scripture. There is a clear claim to its existence and that it is the destination of everyone who does not accept Jesus Christ as their Lord and Savior. From an evidential perspective, we are concerned with whether or not the existence of Hell is incompatible with God. The concept of Hell falls into the category of the *Existence of Evil and Suffering*, which we have already covered. We may not like that Hell exists, but does it serve a purpose that is in line with what we would expect from a loving, just and merciful God?

For this chapter, we have to start with the assumption that God exists and that humans have souls that will extend into eternity. We must be able to test whether or not the characteristics applied to God make sense in light of an eternal place of torment. This perspective might sound odd when you consider that we are actually trying to determine if God exists. Why would we have to assume that he exists before we get started? Simply put, we are testing the compatibility of God and Hell. If God and Hell are not compatible or if it can be shown that there is no way for Hell to exist, then God, Scripture and every truth that Christians hold dear crumbles to the ground.

A Just Destination

Does it make sense that our deeds and decisions during our life would have a consequence? There are four different options when looking at our ultimate destination.

1. Nothing – For everyone. Death is the ultimate end
2. Central Park – For everyone. No Difference between innocence or guilt
3. Judgement
   a. Heaven – For the innocent
   b. Hell – For the guilty

Nothing

All consciousness ends in nothingness. I remember shrugging my shoulders and fatalistically remarking, "When you die you die. Nothingness and dirt. That is it." As an agnostic, I really did not care about eternity or even care about exploring what could be next. It was simply the end, why worry about it. Good and evil have the same destination. Nothing we did while living counted for anything. This view is satisfactory for atheists and agnostics, while unacceptable for the Christian view of eternal souls and a loving and just God.

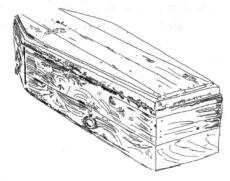

Central Park Equality

What if God turned his back and simply allowed everyone to live for eternity, presumably in peace. This would not be the God of the Bible, but what kind of god would create a place like this? The Central Park destination is nice, but it's not Heaven. As you walk along, Hitler is playing chess with Buddha, and Stalin is painting children's faces. Your sweet grandmother is cutting Mao Tse-Tung's hair, while a platoon from the Khmer Rouge plays volleyball in the sand pit next to the running path.

This scenario would be the eternity congruent with the relativistic, atheistic view of moral values. If there is no transcendent objective moral standard, then Hitler really is morally equal with Gandhi. Justice becomes a concept without meaning because there is nothing to account for. I believe that the eternal Central Park is not possible with an all-loving, just God.

Would not a just God punish Hitler, Stalin and Mao for the millions of murders for which they were responsible? Is it conceivable to anyone's sense of justice that God would let these men enjoy eternity without any consequence for their earthly evil? In the same way, would anyone be satisfied that Mother Teresa and Martin Luther King not be rewarded for their lives of service and sacrifice? I do not believe that anyone would be content accepting an ambivalent god like this.

Neither of the first two options agree with the Biblical description of our possible eternal destinations. The Bible describes God as all loving, merciful and just. The Bible does promise us a destination of Heaven or Hell.

Justice

Would a loving and just God allow evil people to go unpunished? We all have a strong sense of justice. Many of our deepest hurts come from injustices that we have suffered. It is common for us to avoid topics of politics and religion when in a social gathering because they can become so contentious. The root of our intense emotions lies in our innate sense of right and wrong. It does not matter which side of an argument you are on, we will typically agree on the principles that drive our emotions.

The famous OJ Simpson murder trial pitted people who wanted a guilty man to be punished against those who wanted an innocent man to be vindicated. Both of those goals are noble and compatible. Certainly, everyone could agree that they wanted whatever person was truly guilty to be punished. We are naturally saddened by examples of injustice such as the case of Christopher Abernathy:

> *"On October 3, 1984, 15-year-old Kristina Hickey disappeared while walking home from a high school choir performance. Her body was found two days later behind a shopping mall. She had been sexually assaulted and stabbed. After more than 40 hours of interrogation, Christopher Abernathy, a high school dropout who had been classified as learning disabled, signed a confession. Almost immediately, Abernathy recanted the confession and said he signed the statement because police told him he could go home to his mother if he did. No forensic or physical evidence connected Abernathy to the crime." Nearly 30 years later after an independent journalist began uncovering problems with the evidence, the case was reopened and when no trace of Abernathy's DNA was found on the evidence, he was released from prison.* [c]

Our sense of justice is the child of our sense of morals. Our morals reveal to us what is right and wrong, good and evil. Our sense of justice demands consequences for those who do wrong and evil. Without transcendent objective morals, however, our sense of justice is a meaningless force. It is a lightbulb without electricity, an engine without gas.

Our society punishes people like Ted Bundy, for brutally murdering dozens of young women. The descriptions of his acts are disturbing, and they were carried out on young women from families like yours and mine. She was "a tall, slender beautiful girl with long dark hair and blue eyes. She had grown up in a sheltered middle-upper class home near Seattle. She sang beautifully, but her real love was working with mentally handicapped children." Another "was one of six children, and worked two full-time jobs seven days a week the summer before her freshman year, to pay for tuition." And another was, "a newlywed of a year and a half.[ci] Ted Bundy had to be punished!

We turn on the news and instinctively yearn for justice for victims and punishment for criminals and we are pained when justice is not performed. 1 Corinthians 13:6 says love "does not rejoice about injustice but rejoices whenever the truth wins out."

> On August 28, 1955, Emmett Louis Till, a 14 year old black boy was kidnapped and brutally beaten by two white men. The men, Roy Bryant and J. W. Milam "drove for several miles along the river looking for a place to dispose of Till. They shot him by the river and weighted his body"[cii] before dumping him in the river. "In November 1955, a grand jury declined to indict Bryant and Milam for kidnapping, despite the testimony given that they had admitted taking Till." And other witnesses "who testified to seeing Milam enter the shed from which screams and blows were heard."[ciii] Bryant and Milam later confessed to the murder, but were never tried again.

The truth did not win out in this case. Is that the end of it? If someone who is truly guilty is found not-guilty on earth does that define justice for eternity? Is there no eternal justice? Should we expect that God will rectify things upon his jugement? We have laws that govern our society, but what governs eternal justice? If God is a just God, then he will have a mechanism for justice and vindication. As the source of morals and the sole judge, it is his justice system in which we find ourselves.

Is something moral or innocent just because it is legal? In Muslim countries homosexuals face death if they are caught. Is killing homosexuals ok because it is legal? What about the killing of children? It is legal in America to kill unborn human children. Does that make it ok in God's judgement?

Judgement

Every one of us hates injustice and rejoices when the truth wins out. A just God would meet his need for justice by being the final judge, the eternal judge. While on earth we have limited capabilities to determine truth. We can see evidence and make our best determinations, but many times the cases are incomplete and cannot be judged beyond a reasonable doubt. Fortunately, the God described in the Bible is all knowing. His judgements are not based on partial facts or impressions; they are based on a complete and accurate set of evidence.

> *"12 For the word of God is alive and active. Sharper than any double-edged sword, it penetrates even to dividing soul and spirit, joints and marrow; it judges the thoughts and attitudes of the heart. 13 Nothing in all creation is hidden from God's sight. Everything is uncovered and laid bare before the eyes of him to whom we must give account."[civ]*

We can then have faith that the judgement that God passes on each of us, and those for whom we believe deserve punishment is the correct decision. This is both comforting and disturbing. I am struck by the finality of the decision. There is a time for us that *is* too late. There are no defense arguments when we face God. When I spoke earlier of my personal conviction that I could not trust my own judgement about myself, it was in recognition that there was an actual true judgement of who I was. God is that true judge.

So God's judgement is comforting because it is true. Those who deserve punishment will receive punishment and those who deserve vindication will receive vindication. God's judgement is disturbing because it is final and eternal. If you find yourself on the wrong side of God's judgement, there are no second chances and your eternal destination is Hell.

I believe that most non-Christians find difficulty in the exclusivity of the Christian claim that the only way to God's vindication is through Christ. "Why are Christians so arrogant as to say that I will go to Hell if I do not accept Jesus Christ as my savior? I am a good person and there are millions of good people who do not believe in Jesus whom they say will go to Hell."

In future chapters we will deal with the reliability of the Bible and the exclusivity claims of Christianity. We can agree that Jesus either rose from the dead and ascended to heaven or he did not. If you can allow for the assertion at this point that the eternal justice system belongs to God, then we can establish that a just God would have a place to separate the innocent from the guilty. The existence of Hell is just for the guilty and the existence of Heaven is loving towards the innocent.

Mercy

The God of the Bible is claimed to be a merciful God. The entire Bible revolves around the redemption plan freely available for all of us.

> *"For God so loved the world that he gave his one and only Son, that whoever believes in him shall not perish but have eternal life. [17] For God did not send his Son into the world to condemn the world, but to save the world through him." – John 3:16-17*

It seems merciful that God would provide a way to avoid Hell. Hell is described in the Bible as a "blazing furnace, where there will be weeping and gnashing of teeth."[cv] And those destined for Hell "will drink the wine of God's fury, which has been poured full strength into the cup of his wrath. They will be tormented with burning sulfur."[cvi] Anyone who believes the Bible would want to avoid this destination and anyone looking at the Christian worldview should be moved to acknowledge God's mercifulness in allowing a way to avoid it.

In the story of the rich man and the beggar, we get another glimpse of the type of torment people will experience in Hell. The rich man in Hell begs Abraham,

> 27 *"He answered, 'Then I beg you, father, send Lazarus to my family, 28 for I have five brothers. Let him warn them, so that they will not also come to this place of torment.' 29 "Abraham replied, 'They have Moses and the Prophets; let them listen to them.' 30 "'No, father Abraham,' he said, 'but if someone from the dead goes to them, they will repent.' 31 "He said to him, 'If they do not listen to Moses and the Prophets, they will not be convinced even if someone rises from the dead.'" - Luke 16:27-31*

The mental anguish of regret and conscious fear for loved ones left behind will tear at people for eternity. How much more pain did this rich man experience as his brothers arrived in Hell one after the other?

Torment is not torture. It is clear that Hell is an intolerable place, but it is never described in the Bible as torture. We do not understand the full nature of Hell, but we know that it is desirable to avoid it at all costs, even if the path to redemption seems distasteful to you.

People complain about the exclusivity of Christ without examining the evidence for Christ. God has opened up his Kingdom to those who hold the key. God only made one key for his home and he gives copies out freely to everyone who asks. He chose Christ as that key. Jesus answered, "I am the way and the truth and the life. No one comes to the Father except through me."[cvii] – John 14:6

Taking a Breath

Why is it wrong for God to offer mercy to everyone? We have already shown how the existence of Hell is consistent with a loving and just God. What person would not want this God to also offer a path to clemency? If God has the right to judge, and we want God to impose judgement, shouldn't we welcome any offer of mercy with thanks and rejoicing?

According to the Bible, God's offer of forgiveness is an offer to regain our innocence under his judgement. The ability for us to have innocence was gained through the death, burial and resurrection of Jesus Christ. Christ was innocent, and freely carried our guilt to the cross. He endured God's judgement of our guilt in order to pay the eternal price for us. God asks you to accept that free gift of salvation by recognizing Jesus Christ as your Lord and Savior. That is mercy.

> *"For this reason Christ is the mediator of a new covenant, that those who are called may receive the promised eternal inheritance—now that he has died as a ransom to set them free from the sins committed under the first covenant."[cviii]- Hebrews 9:14-16*

Does it make sense that we would reject this offer because we dislike the principle of it? If there is a fire consuming your hotel would you reject exiting through the servants' area because it was socially unacceptable? What would you think of the person standing at the top of the stairs asserting their disgust with the lower classes and with those who are willingly lowering themselves to that level in order to save themselves? I am saying to that person, "You can hold onto your repulsion, but please allow me to show you that it is the only way to escape the fire." The offer of salvation through Jesus Christ seems absurd to some, but I would suggest that is before examining the evidence.

Good Enough

When we face God and he truly judges our lives in accordance with complete knowledge of the truth, each and every one of us will deserve to be found guilty. None of us on our own will achieve the perfection necessary to claim innocence. Each of us has taken advantage of our free will to do wrong, to be selfish, to lie, to steal and to hurt. Our life's list of deeds does not work on a balance. Two good deeds does not make up for one bad deed. Any sin qualifies us as guilty.

The mercy that God offers through Christ is that if you accept Christ's sacrifice for your sins, God will apply your sins to Christ in that judgement and find you innocent.

In this salvation scenario, it is important to realize that a *good* person without Christ is not a good person. Gandhi may have been a *good* person – a *great* person, but how serious do you think God took his rejection of Christ? God communicated with the world through Scripture, which we examined in a previous chapter, and provided very specific instructions for salvation. Gandhi said in essence, "I reject this god and his message. I reject what god said about Christ." In doing so, he became responsible for all of the un-good[cix] things he did and was found guilty before God. This same logic applies to your sweet aunt Millie, and to you and me.

Duration

There are lots of reasons to be repulsed by Hell and one of the most troublesome is the eternal nature of the place. Why would guilt from our limited time on earth have to be paid for forever? J. Warner Wallace explains that the length of the punishment is tied to the severity of the crime not the length of time it takes to commit the crime.[cx] God gives us our lifetimes to determine our choice for eternity. The rejection of

	Jesus	No Jesus
Vote	☐	☐

God, his message and his Son are eternal choices which carry eternal consequences.[cxi] I cannot answer why God would not give a second chance after we die, but he doesn't.

> *But he has appeared once for all at the culmination*
> *of the ages to do away with sin by the sacrifice of*

himself. [27] Just as people are destined to die once, and after that to face judgment, [28] so Christ was sacrificed once to take away the sins of many;[cxii] - Hebrews 9:26-28

The opportunity to examine the evidence for God's creation and his plan for salvation is clearly available to you. Your free-will decision to accept or reject Christ will be respected by God for eternity.

Hell

From a Christian perspective, Hell is a very real place. It is a place that is compatible with an all-loving, just and merciful God. Any scenario for eternity which does not include a place for justice would be a scenario that anyone would consider falsely optimistic and unsatisfactory since evil would not be repaid.

Implications of Each Conclusion

Believing that Hell does not exist is the naturalistic view of the world. You accept the eternal meaninglessness of your life and everyone else's life. Whether you do good or bad in life is of no consequence. You are rejecting any eternity, any scripture, any truth and any mercy as unnecessary. Though you desire justice, if someone gets away with something while they are alive, then good for them.

Believing that Hell exists carries with it the Christian God and enteral justice and mercy. You accept your guilt and your inability to attain innocence on your own. You accept God's eternal plan, which includes a merciful path to your innocence.

Note: It is possible to believe in eternity without being a Christian, but it carries with it some difficulties. You may think that you are good enough to enter Heaven without following Christ and you deny the necessity for atonement for your sin or you believe that there is some other path to atonement. You try to be a good person. Perhaps you make the free-will choice to accept Hell as your destination in open rebellion to God's word and plan.

> Answer the Assessment questions from the
> beginning of the chapter again

Characteristics of the Free Will Giver

- Loving
- Eternal
- Just
- Merciful

Deliverables

- Our sense of Justice is like our moral sense. For it to mean anything, it must come from an external source.
- God is a just God who will not allow the guilty to go free.
- God is a loving God who will reward the innocent.
- God is a merciful God who has provided a path to innocence.
- From God's perspective, no one is good who rejects him and his plan for redemption through Jesus Christ.

CHAPTER 11

Prophecy

Is Prophecy Real?

Possible Conclusions

1. No. Prophecy is not real. Supposed prophecy was written after the events happened or the fulfillment of the prophecy was made up.

2. Yes. Prophecy is real. Prophecy has been fulfilled with perfection throughout Scripture.

Assessment

Question	Before Reading	After Reading
Prophecy cannot be tested.	Y/T - N/F	Y/T - N/F
The Old Testament and New Testament are different parts of the same story.	Y/T - N/F	Y/T - N/F
The Old Testament was finished shortly after Jesus' death.	Y/T - N/F	Y/T - N/F
Jesus knew the Old Testament prophecies and purposely fulfilled them to convince people that he was the messiah.	Y/T - N/F	Y/T - N/F
There is no prophecy of the messiah that is specific enough to definitely identify Jesus.	Y/T - N/F	Y/T - N/F
If prophecy actually happened it would count as a miracle.	Y/T - N/F	Y/T - N/F

Prophecy Introduction

We were seated facing the ground one second and then the next we were looking straight into the sky. The Huey Helicopter flew just above the Nisqually River following every curve. The noise was all encompassing as the wind and rotor sounds rushed through the open doors. Our rifles were pointed downward with the muzzles resting on the floor between our feet and a single lap-belt held us in place as the helicopter swooped from side to side. For all intents and purposes, we were soldiers going to war in some foreign jungle.

The helicopter should not fly – except that it does. Helicopters are described as a group of spare parts flying in close proximity to each other. When you look at a helicopter sitting on the ground, it looks like a rock with an umbrella skeleton sticking out of the top. If you threw a tarp over the rotor blades  you could have a nice picnic in the shade. Though the design looks like it is opposed to flight, helicopters fly because they were, in fact, designed to fly.

Every component of the helicopter must be working in order for it to stay airborne. The rotor must be turning at the proper speed and the blades at the proper angle. The hydraulics must be pumping at the proper pressure and speed. The tail rotor must be turning and responsive. So, as odd as the system looks, it is actually an incredibly intricate machine that works perfectly together. Without some orientation, however, it is hard to see how one piece relates to the other and how there are overlaps in effects of one thing acting on another that give it capabilities that no other type of aircraft has.

I was not thinking about the impossibility of the helicopter flying as I was enjoying the surreal experience of looking straight down at the river from 100 feet in the air, engulfed in the environment. I trusted the aircraft and I trusted the pilots. I was enjoying the ride.

Prophecy is part of what binds the seemingly unwieldy Bible into an aerodynamic masterpiece. Prophecy is like the wiring of the Bible running through every component from the main rotors' angle to the speed of the tail rotor and everything in between. If prophecy were not part of the Bible, the "spare parts flying in close proximity," would fall from the sky.

Paul warns us in 1 Thessalonians 5:20 [20] "Do not treat prophecies with contempt [21] but test them all."

Exploring Prophecy

Telling the future is impossible so any claim that it has been done is false and requires no additional discussion. We look at people claiming to know the future as kooks or swindlers. We even look at those using *science* to predict the future as sketchy when we get to look back to evaluate the failure of their predictions. Al Gore's credibility has dwindled as the predictions from his 2006 movie, *An Inconvenient Truth*, fail to materialize. Kilimanjaro still has snow year round, no statistically significant warming has occurred, weather hasn't gotten worse and the North Pole still has ice.[cxiii] Al Gore, like anyone claiming to be a prophet, is brave to the extent that they make themselves vulnerable to testing.

If the prophecy comes true, then they were a prophet; if it does not come true, then they were not a prophet. The Bible uses this fact as a way of identifying real prophets from false prophets.

> *[21] You may say to yourselves, "How can we know when a message has not been spoken by the Lord?"*
> *[22] If what a prophet proclaims in the name of the Lord does not take place or come true, that is a message the Lord has not spoken. That prophet has spoken presumptuously, so do not be alarmed. –*
> *Deuteronomy 18:21-22*

The Old Testament subjected itself to falsification. The majority of its prophecies would not come to pass for hundreds of years. We know what we think of false prophets, but what should we make of prophets that make predictions that do come true?

It's fair to be skeptical of prophecy and to investigate whether or not it is possible. When evaluating what is true and what is false, we need to determine:

1. Was it written before the event it describes?
2. Has it been modified after the event?
3. Was it really fulfilled? Generic prophecies are rather worthless, so we want to know how specific they were and how verifiable the fulfillment of them is.

The Old Testament

The Old Testament of the Bible is made up of the original Jewish Scriptures. The books of the Old Testament were written from 1600 BC – 400 BC by 31 authors in several different places from The Saini, to Jerusalem to Babylon. Two of the major prophetic books are the book of Isaiah, written before 696 BC and Daniel, written before 530 BC. I emphasize that Scripture means sacred, authoritative writing and BC stands for Before Christ. The Jews were carefully compiling and carrying around what they considered to be sacred writings hundreds of years before Christ walked the earth. And, to tie things together, Christ translated to Hebrew means Anointed One and Messiah.

Written Before the Events and Accurately Transmitted Through Time

The evidence supporting the early writing and accurate transmittal of the document through time is extraordinarily strong. The entire set of Hebrew Scripture was translated into Greek between 300-200 BC by 70 scholars. The document is known as the Septuagint.[cxiv] Then, the Dead Sea Scrolls, including the entire book of Isaiah, were discovered and verified to have been copied at least 100 years BC. On the bulletin board of time, the Old Testament and the prophecies it contains were hanging there well before Christ.[cxv]

The same evidence noting the early authorship of the Old Testament prophecies also supports the accurate transmittal of the documents through time. Even the quoting of the Old Testament by

New Testament authors would be evidence against the reliability of the documents should they be found to be inaccurate by new archeological discoveries.

People today do not realize that the disciples did not know that their credibility would be questioned with regard to the Old Testament. They quoted the Old Testament frequently in total confidence that they were doing it accurately because that is the Scripture that they had. They convinced thousands of Jews who were students of the same Scripture that Jesus was the Messiah prophesized in their Scripture. They could not have done so with false teaching – teaching that can be held up to scrutiny even today! The Dead Sea Scrolls, found in 1947, simply add to our comfort that these Scriptures were, in fact, in place well before Christ.

What Was Written?

My challenge for this section is limiting what to include. There are estimates of 300 Old-Testament Prophecies that point to the Messiah (Christ). As I read the prophecies, each one seems better than the last, but I'll stick to my purpose of providing prophecies that are specific. Remember that you are reading words that were verified to have been written hundreds of years before Christ.

Remainder of page intentionally left blank so the next section could be read on one page.

Read this column first. Seven hundred years before Christ, Isaiah, contained in the Old Testament, wrote: (New testament references in parentheses)	Read this column second. The New Testament references from the first column precede its verse. Christ's purpose and death were described:
Chapter 53. [4] Surely he took up our pain and bore our suffering, (Ephesians 1:7) yet we considered him punished by God, stricken by him, and afflicted.(Matthew 27:26) [5] But he was pierced for our transgressions, he was crushed for our iniquities; (Matthew 27:31) the punishment that brought us peace was on him, and by his wounds we are healed. [6] We all, like sheep, have gone astray, each of us has turned to our own way; and the Lord has laid on him the iniquity of us all. [7] He was oppressed and afflicted, yet he did not open his mouth; he was led like a lamb to the slaughter, and as a sheep before its shearers is silent, so he did not open his mouth. (Matthew 27:12-14) [8] By oppression and judgment he was taken away. Yet who of his generation protested? (Mark 14:50) For he was cut off from the land of the living; for the transgression of my people he was punished. (Hebrews 9:28) [9] He was assigned a grave with the wicked, and with the rich in his death, (Matthew 27:57-60) though he had done no violence, nor was any deceit in his mouth.	(Mark 14:50) Then everyone deserted him and fled. (Matthew 27:12-14) When he was accused by the chief priests and the elders, he gave no answer. Then Pilate asked him, "Do not you hear the testimony they are bringing against you?" But Jesus made no reply, not even to a single charge—to the great amazement of the governor. (Matthew 27:19) Pilate's wife sent him this message: "Do not have anything to do with that innocent man." (Matthew 27:26) Pilate had Jesus flogged. (Matthew 27:31) After they had mocked him, they led him away to crucify him. (John 1:11) He came to that which was his own, but his own did not receive him. (Hebrews 9:28) so Christ was sacrificed once to take away the sins of many; (Ephesians 1:7) In him we have redemption through his blood, the forgiveness of sins, (Matthew 27:57-60) As evening approached, there came a rich man who asked for Jesus' body, and Pilate ordered that it be given to him for burial.[cxvi]

There are vast numbers of descriptions of Christ's life and death in the New Testament illustrating how Isaiah's prophecies were precisely fulfilled. It is one thing for a person to purposely fulfill a prediction, such as when Jesus went to the synagogue in his hometown of Nazareth and read from the book of Isaiah regarding the Messiah and then said, "Today this scripture is fulfilled in your hearing."[cxvii] Any one of us could walk into a church pick up a Bible, choose an appropriate verse from the Book of Revelation, "The armies of heaven were following him, riding on white horses," and then claim "I am the rider."[cxviii] However, we'd soon be called a fool even if we yelled, "Charge!" and ran out the front door and jumped onto our white stallion and rode off.

Jesus, however, was pin-pointed in history from his lineage, to his place of birth, to where he would grow up (which was different than where he was born). He was identified from his death as a criminal assigned a grave with the wicked to his burial in a rich man's tomb. The nature of the life and the ministry of the prophesized Messiah were matched in his life perfectly, including how and when he would be revealed as the Messiah.

When was the Messiah Supposed to Come?
I was driving down the road in 2003 listening to a recording of my favorite Bible teacher, Chuck Missler. He was taking me through verses 24-27 of the 9th chapter of the book of Daniel. The passages are commonly called *Daniel's 70 Weeks*. When you listen to Dr. Missler you have to pay attention because he draws things on the blackboard of your mind and connects them in dramatic ways. I was used to him surprising me with biblical insights that can only be known if you study the Old and New Testaments together. On this particular day, when he landed the knockout punch of his lesson, my blood ran cold.

Daniel wrote at about 530 BC. Nearly 100 years later, Nehemiah recorded events. Daniel predicted that "From the time the word goes out to restore and rebuild Jerusalem until the Anointed One, the ruler, comes, there will be" 483 years.[cxix]

Nehemiah chapter two describes the command that King Artaxerxes gave to rebuild Jerusalem and its wall. This started the clock on Daniel's prophecy. The date was March 14, 445 BC[cxx]

On April 6, 32 AD, Mark chapter 11 tells us that Jesus entered Jerusalem on a donkey and allowed himself to be identified as the Messiah for the first time. This stopped the clock on Daniel's prophecy. The Pharisees protested,

39 "Teacher, rebuke your disciples!"

40 "I tell you," he replied, "if they keep quiet, the stones will cry out."

41 As he approached Jerusalem and saw the city, he wept over it 42 and said, "If you, even you, had only known on this day what would bring you peace—but now it is hidden from your eyes.

In his Book, *The Coming Prince*, Sir Robert Anderson walks through the calendars as they existed from 530 BC through 32 AD to identify the exact dates and years that the prophesized events occurred and the number of days between them since years were 360 days long when Daniel prophesized the events. The prophesied number of days was 173,880 (483 years X 360 days). Chuck Missler writes, "When we examine the period between March 14, 445 BC and April 6, 32 AD, and correct for leap years, we discover that it is 173,880 days exactly, to the very day!"cxxi

When searching for specific prophecy, there is none more precise than this one.

Just in Time

Jesus came when predicted, and as it turns out it was at precisely the right time. If Daniel's prophecies were off by 10%, Jesus would have shown up in 80 AD, 10 years after the Temple was destroyed. That may not seem like a big deal, but when another prophecy relies on the existence of the Temple in order to be fulfilled, it is a very big deal. Malachi 3:1 written about 400 BC prophesizes,

> *"Then suddenly the Lord you are seeking will come to his temple; the messenger of the covenant, whom you desire, will come," says the Lord Almighty.*

Yes, Jesus fulfilled that prophecy in Mark 11:15

> *[15] On reaching Jerusalem, Jesus entered the temple courts and began driving out those who were buying and selling there.*

Internal Proof for the Reliability of Scripture

The connection between the Old Testament and the New Testament is like a tree. In the roots of the Old Testament lie the prediction of the branches, leaves and fruit. The plan of God's creation and redemption of mankind that started in the Garden of Eden predicted the redeemer and the reconciliation of the creation to God. The words flow like nutrients from one to the other and the sunlight works to strengthen the entire body.

I may have gotten a little poetic there, but the point is that God's plan and his revelation of that plan make one coherent system – one tree.

The existence of this evidence of knowledge originating outside of time is independent of other arguments for the existence of God. No matter what your choice was with regard to the creation of the Universe or life, you are faced with the knowledge that there is stunning evidence for fulfilled prophecy of the Bible and that it exists in abundance. The Bible itself shows the evidence of being a supernaturally inspired work. The fulfilled prophecy is also strong evidence for miracles.

What's Next?

If you were exploring a shipwreck from the 1600's and found a box hidden under debris, you'd be anxious to get to the surface and open it. When you do, you discover that it contains 30 stones each with a name and number on it. You line up the stones from 1 – 30 only to realize that it lists the winners of the Baseball World Series in order starting in the year 2000. Baseball did not even exist in the 1600s and yet there is no mistake. The stone representing this year reads "Red Birds." Which team to you put your money on this year?

From an evidential standpoint, we must look at prophecy that has either been fulfilled or that which has been proven false. In the case where we have a book that presents itself as prophetic and it has been 100% accurate to this point, what do we do with the prophecies that are yet to be fulfilled? In the same way you would put your money on the Cardinals in the World Series this year, you would trust in the knowledge that has proven itself to be outside of time.

The prophecies that have not yet been fulfilled from both the Old Testament and New Testament refer to the end times. There are hundreds of interconnected predictions about how God will bring about his final judgement. How amazing would it be to discover what the Bible says about the Rapture of the Christian Church, the rise of the anti-Christ, the peace he brings and the Great Tribulation that follows? When will Jesus come again, what does his earthly reign look like and where will those who worship Him live?

Revelation 22:7 [7]"Look, I am coming soon! Blessed is the one who keeps the words of the prophecy written in this scroll."

Implications of Each Conclusion

Believing that prophecy was falsified in some way gives you relief from recognizing the Bible as inspired by a knowledge that is outside of time. You are then able to deny any of its teaching and pursue whatever belief system you wish to adopt. You ignore the evidence knowing that there are prophecies yet to be fulfilled that claim to impact the eternal destination of every person.

Believing that the Old Testament contains prophecy that was precisely fulfilled in the life, death and resurrection of Christ should give you confidence in his identity and purpose. We can know that God is revealed to be outside of time and governing his plan for your redemption. You can have peace knowing that God has been preparing your eternity from the beginning.

> Answer the Assessment questions from the
> beginning of the chapter again

Characteristics of the Prophecy Giver
- Outside of Time
- All Knowing
- Loving

Deliverables
- The Old Testament was completed hundreds of years before Jesus was born.
- The Old Testament was started in 1600 BC and finished by 400 BC.
- The OT is verified accurate through the Septuagint and the Dead Sea Scrolls.
- The Old Testament foretold nearly all aspects of Jesus' identity, life, purpose, death and resurrection.
- Daniel prophesized Jesus revealing as the Messiah to the day.
- Prophecy ties the Old and New Testaments together.
- Fulfilled prophecy is strong proof for the reliability of Scripture and miracles.
- If the Bible has been accurate up until now, we can have faith that the prophecies yet to be fulfilled are accurate as well.

CHAPTER 12

Miracles

Are Miracles Possible?

Possible Conclusions

1. No. Miracles are not possible. Miracles are outside of the possibility of natural forces, which are the only forces that exist.
2. Yes. Miracles are possible. Miracles are the result of the plan and action of God. God imposes his will on natural forces in order to bring about a miracle. The Bible is full of examples of miracles that actually happened.

Assessment

Question	Before Reading	After Reading
Natural forces cannot be changed.	Y/T - N/F	Y/T - N/F
Miracles were used by God to identify Jesus as the Christ.	Y/T - N/F	Y/T - N/F
Miracles are really just very strange events caused by an odd interaction of natural forces.	Y/T - N/F	Y/T - N/F
When science learns more we will see how supposed miracles really happened.	Y/T - N/F	Y/T - N/F

Miracles Introduction

Even though it was summer in Thailand, I had to sleep with my head underneath the blanket. It was really hot and really humid. I could feel and hear the tap-tap of bugs hitting the blanket as the rotating ceiling fan blew them onto me. Everyone except for the General that I worked for was in the same situation in the barracks. There was no air conditioning, no room service, and no relief from the heat at night. We simply had a cot, a blanket and a ceiling fan.

The General, on the other hand was staying in a very nice hotel room. I remember the golden motif of the room and lounge area. The air conditioning was a bit too cold, but refreshing none-the-less. The remains of the General's breakfast were on the table, and he allowed me to pour a cup of coffee for myself from the carafe. That is the way it works in the Army. As you rise in the ranks some of the nicer amenities are provided for you.

The important part of rising in the ranks was the added authority and responsibility that come with the position. Though the General was able to rest in a more comfortable place than me he carried a much heavier burden of responsibility. The Army respects the criticality of getting the mission accomplished and it creates a culture where authority is respected and obeyed. When the General ordered a task be accomplished, it was not an optional request. With respect to the leadership principle of listening to input from others, when the time came to move, it was the leader's decision and we all moved.

The Thai Generals and American leaders worked together during the joint military exercise. Each had their staff working in large rooms filled with tables and boards and they scheduled conferences to determine plans and actions. The leaders moved units around and gave orders to them just as you would expect, and when they wanted to travel by helicopter, they summoned their aids to call ahead to the helipad to get the chopper geared up. Millions of dollars of equipment and hundreds of soldiers covering a large portion of the southern portion of Thailand were under their command.

A sign of authority is how people respond to your orders. Any of us could observe a group of people accomplishing a task and determine who had authority just by what they said and how others responded. The sign of obedience from others identifies them as the one with authority. Those with greater authority are able to direct greater resources. CEOs can move companies and Presidents can move countries.

What would we make of the person to whom the laws of nature are obedient?

Exploring Miracles

We are going to get philosophical in this lesson. But before we do you should remember one thing, if God is possible, miracles are possible. Miracles are a topic revolving around the supernatural, things beyond the natural laws that govern the Universe. When people argue against miracles, they are not really arguing against God. People who argue against the possibility of miracles have already decided that there is no God. They absolutely must take this position before they start talking because with the possibility of God comes the possibility of miracles.

We have been dealing with miracles from the beginning of this book and we have seen what happens when naturalists pre-suppose – decide ahead of time – that there is no God. They work themselves into contortions with which most of us would be uncomfortable.

- Miracle #1 - The Creation: Theoretical Physicist, Lawrence Krauss says that the nothing from which the Universe came is not really nothing. Nothing does not really mean nothing.[cxxii]
- Miracle #2 - Fine Tuning: Neil deGrasse Tyson and many others, say that there are an infinite number of universes (multi-verse) and that the incredible precision of dozens of forces are a fortunate accident. The multi-verse may have been created by superior alien beings.[cxxiii]
- Miracle #3 - Life from non-life: Evolutionists say that chemical information organized itself into a self-replicating, self-protecting system and continued to randomly add complexity and information until it all made sense. Science says that life only comes from life today, but they believe that at some point in the past that law did not apply and life came from non-life.
- Miracle #4 - Evolution: Evolutionary biologist, Richard Dawkins says you should ignore the *apparent* design and unbelievable complexity and believe that massive amounts of time and countless random biological changes created the life we see today.[cxxiv]

We have spent the previous chapters evaluating the evidence that supports and refutes the existence of God. If you have decided that there is no God, then there are no miracles. Done! If you are all in for God or are still undecided, then let's get philosophical.

Miracles are the observable acts of the supernatural. Raising someone from the dead is an act of the *supernatural* in the same way sitting up in bed is a *natural* act of ours. No one would argue that throwing our feet over the side of the bed has supernatural causes, however, to reject any act as being supernaturally caused is extreme in the other direction. Unfortunately, skeptics pre-suppose that the supernatural does not exist before they have performed a reasonable examination of the evidence.

David Hume, the 18th Century philosopher claimed that miracles were impossible. He made the point that no matter how good the evidence for miracles, they are simply false due to the supreme standing of the laws of nature. He says that despite what may seem to be insurmountable evidence for a miracle it cannot be true because the laws of nature cannot be overruled. In essence, David Hume tells you, "You may earnestly believe that you witnessed a miracle, but you really did not."cxxv

But what happens when the probability of witness' testimony of a miracle being false would be an even greater miracle than what the witnesses say that they saw? For instance, the disciples know the difference between the living and the dead. These eye witnesses reported that Jesus was alive, then he died, and then he was alive. The resurrection of Jesus would constitute a miracle. It would also be a miracle for these eye witnesses to voluntarily go to their deaths rather than take back their testimony about Jesus. Choose your miracle.

Benedict de Spinoza writing in the 17th Century believed that the laws of nature were actually part of God's nature and therefore unchangeable and God cannot do something against his nature. He says that when accounts of a miracle seem credible they are simply the result of natural forces which we do not yet understand.cxxvi

Other philosophers support the possibility of miracles by demonstrating God's superior relation to natural forces.

> *Samuel Clarke states, "The so-called natural forces*
> *of matter, such as gravitation, are properly speaking*
> *the effect of God's acting on matter at every moment.*
> *...what we discern as the course of nature is nothing*
> *else than God's will, producing certain effects in a*

> *continual and uniform manner. Thus, a miracle is not against the course of nature, which really does not exist, except only insofar as it is an unusual event which God does. Thus, the regular 'works' of nature prove the being and attributes of God, and miracles prove the interposition of God into the regular order in which he acts. "*[cxxvii]

Clarke suggests that the laws of nature are not part of God's nature, but that he is constantly acting to maintain the laws of nature in a steady state. He is fully capable of altering these laws when it is within his will and plan.

> *The laws of nature "depend on the will of God, and it is only the constant and uniform procession of the normal course of nature that leads us to think it is invariable. God does not change nature's course entirely, but can make exceptions to the general rules when he deems it important. These miracles serve to show that the course of nature 'is not the effect of a blind necessity, but of a free Cause who interrupts and suspends it when he pleases.'"*[cxxviii]

We have three choices before us.
1) No God – no miracles,
2) Laws of nature and God's nature are the same and cannot change – no miracles,
3) God is superior to the laws of nature and can perform miracles.

If you accept that there is no God, then you can stop here. Fold these pages into airplanes and cranes and go about your business. The difference between 2 and 3 is God's relation to the laws of nature. If you go back and review the chapter on fine tuning, I believe you will find that the laws of nature are not required to be their current values. These forces could very well be at different values. The laws of nature are set, but they could very well have been set at different, life-prohibiting values. Besides that, God is the one who put those values into the Universe to govern the relationship between time, space and matter. God is the God of the laws of nature too.

What Good are Miracles?

If we can accept that miracles can't prove or disprove God, we should be able accept that if there is a God, he is superior to natural laws. If God created the Universe and input the perfectly balanced set of natural laws, then he is superior to those laws. We have spent the book getting to the point where you can accept miracles as an expected part of God's work. Did these miracles happen by accident or is there a design to them like everything else we suggest God did?

Miracles Identify Jesus

Wait, what just happened? Who did what? Who does that kind of thing? As he prepared to raise Lazarus from the dead,

> *[41] Jesus looked up and said, "Father, I thank you that you have heard me. [42] I knew that you always hear me, but I said this for the benefit of the people standing here, that they may believe that you sent me." [43] When he had said this, Jesus called in a loud voice, "Lazarus, come out!" [44] The dead man came out." – John 11:41-44*

Jesus had to have a lot of patience with his followers. We can see him coming to the tomb and taking the time to pray out loud for the benefit of those standing around. He did not do it because he had to. He did it as evidence for us.

> *[2] When John, who was in prison, heard about the deeds of the Messiah, he sent his disciples [3] to ask him, "Are you the one who is to come, or should we expect someone else?" [4] Jesus replied, "Go back and report to John what you hear and see: [5] The blind receive sight, the lame walk, those who have leprosy are cleansed, the deaf hear, the dead are raised, and the good news is proclaimed to the poor. – Matthew 11:2-5*

The purpose of the miracles was heeded by some. Jesus was identified as the one God sent, as the Messiah as a direct result of the miracles he had performed. Then, on that 173,880[th] day when he first allowed himself to be publicly identified as the Messiah,

> *37 When he came near the place where the road goes down the Mount of Olives, the whole crowd of disciples began joyfully to praise God in loud voices for all the miracles they had seen: 38 "Blessed is the king who comes in the name of the Lord!" – Luke 19:37-38*

But the Jewish leaders did not accept Jesus, and Jesus held them responsible for their choice to reject the evidence he provided.

> *41 As he approached Jerusalem and saw the city, he wept over it 42 and said, "If you, even you, had only known on this day what would bring you peace—but now it is hidden from your eyes. – Luke 19:41-42*

Jesus knew that miracles were so powerful he promised harsh judgement for those who willfully ignored the evidence before them.

> *20 Then Jesus began to denounce the towns in which most of his miracles had been performed, because they did not repent. 21 "Woe to you, Chorazin! Woe to you, Bethsaida! For if the miracles that were performed in you had been performed in Tyre and Sidon, they would have repented long ago in sackcloth and ashes. 22 But I tell you, it will be more bearable for Tyre and Sidon on the day of judgment than for you. 23 And you, Capernaum, will you be lifted to the heavens? No, you will go down to Hades. For if the miracles that were performed in you had been performed in Sodom, it would have remained to this day. 24 But I tell you that it will be more bearable for Sodom on the day of judgment than for you." – Matthew 11:20-24*

Peter's first words after receiving the Holy Spirt was to identify Christ as the Messiah by quoting prophecy fulfilled by the coming of the Holy Spirit and by claiming that Jesus was verified as the Messiah by the miracles he performed.

> [22] *"Fellow Israelites, listen to this: Jesus of Nazareth was a man accredited by God to you by miracles, wonders and signs, which God did among you through him, as you yourselves know. – Acts 2:22*

You are a contestant on Wheel of Fortune, Pat Sajak says, "Vanna, do we have any miracles in this phrase?"

"Yes. There are 11 miracles in this phrase."

Pat looks to you and asks, "For a trip to eternity, what does it spell?"

You have a big smile on your face as you say, "Jesus is Lord."

Every miracle Christ did was another indicator of who he was. It was God answering our human desire for proof. We would test a supposed messiah today, "if you are God, perform a miracle." Yet we already have reliable scripture, validated by the miracles of fulfilled prophecy and reports of miracles performed by the man claiming to the Messiah. At what point do we accept Christ's word for who he said he was? Would one more miracle do the trick? Would an appearance of Jesus healing people in the downtown mall make a difference?

Abraham listened to the rich man beg for a messenger to be sent to his living relatives to warn them against the judgement awaiting them if they rejected God.

> [30] *"'No, father Abraham,' he said, 'but if someone from the dead goes to them, they will repent.'* [31] *"Abraham said to him, 'If they do not listen to Moses and the Prophets, they will not be convinced even if someone rises from the dead.'" – Luke 16:30-31*

Implications of Each Conclusion

Believing that miracles are not possible means that you are accepting to not know how seemingly miraculous events have occurred or you are defending wildly improbable events as having happened as a result of natural forces.

Believing that miracles are possible acknowledges the evidence that the most probable cause of certain events is of supernatural origin. You have the burden of showing that natural causes are highly unlikely to be the cause, but not to the point of understanding exactly how they happen.

> Answer the Assessment questions from the
> beginning of the chapter again

Characteristics of the Miracle Maker
1. All Powerful
2. Purposeful

Deliverables
- If God is possible, miracles are possible
- Those who say miracles are not possible assume that there is no God.
- The miracles that atheists believe in are, 1) Something from nothing uncaused, 2) Fine Tuning of the Universe, 3) Life emerging from Non-life, and 4) evolution.
- God is superior to the Natural laws he put in place
- Miracles are used to confirm the identity of Jesus

CHAPTER 13

Resurrection

Did the Resurrection Occur?

Possible Conclusions

1. No. The Resurrection did not occur. The resurrection would be a miracle, which is impossible. The resurrection story originated and was modified from some other set of writings or events.

2. Yes. The Resurrection did occur. Jesus rose from the dead on the third day as was prophesized. Jesus defeated death and is the hope of all Christians.

Assessment

Question	Before Reading	After Reading
The resurrection of Jesus is a myth.	Y/T - N/F	Y/T - N/F
The disciples stole Jesus' body.	Y/T - N/F	Y/T - N/F
The disciples were demoralized when Jesus died.	Y/T - N/F	Y/T - N/F
The disciples became wealthy as the heads of the Christian Church.	Y/T - N/F	Y/T - N/F
The disciples didn't really build the church.	Y/T - N/F	Y/T - N/F
Christianity is very much like Judaism but without the ongoing sacrifices.	Y/T - N/F	Y/T - N/F

Resurrection Introduction

One day I was the average young Army Lieutenant spouting profanity in my everyday language and the next day I stopped. One day I had a quick and hot temper and the next day I did not. I can't remember if both of these instant transformations happened on the same day, but it was definitely within a month of each other.

I was in the middle of what turned out to be my favorite assignment in the Army. I was the RECON platoon leader for an Air Cav Squadron. I had 15 soldiers who lived the motto, "Nothing is too Hard!" My squad leaders were young NCO's and I dealt directly with them. My senior NCO's handled admin and support. I liked it that way.

I was running around with almost no body fat, I could run 'til the cows came home, and do a ruck march with the best of them. The environment was one where profanity was as normal as the coffee we drank. We grew close enough to each other that one of my squad leaders, John Johnson, was later the best man at my wedding. Cursing was normal, even expected, and yet I stopped cold turkey.

My temper was well used in my marriage and amongst some of my troops when they messed up or slacked off. My temper was used as a way of fighting back or dominating another person. In my marriage I had to fight just to stay even and I always kind of felt better when I was meaner or louder or somehow ended with the best point. But I knew it was wrong.

I was in the middle of the first great truth search of my life. I had become drawn to the self-help genre. My study gained emphasis with the destruction of the trust of my wife as I explained in the chapter on morals. I knew I had to be a better person and I was determined to be. I had not yet read the Bible, but I was heading that way.

Truth began to jump out to me as I read the book, *How to Win Friends and Influence People*, by Dale Carnegie.[cxxix] I can't remember the exact wording, but the message was that no one wins an argument even if you are right. I realized I had to stop losing my temper. Then I read another classic, *7 Habits of Highly Successful People*, by Steven Covey.[cxxx] There was a simple diagram on page 71 that had the word "Stimulus" on the left and the word "Response" on the right. Stimulus is what happens to you and response is how you react to it. And the truth that was presented in that diagram was what was pictured between those two words – Choice.

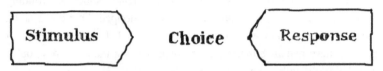

I instantly became a different person because of that diagram. My temper was gone. I did not know what to replace it with yet, but the yelling and anger stopped.

My cursing stopped in the same manner, but as the result of choosing to be professional. The normal opinions offered by *proper* people about cursing had been floating around in my mind for a long time. Profanity is the sign of a limited vocabulary. It is rude and disrespectful. When I accepted the truth and chose to act in accordance with that truth, I stopped cursing immediately.

These transformations took place 30 years ago and I have never gone back. I have had lapses in temper from time to time, but only on a handful of occasions – oh wait – there are more if you count my kids. But to the point, I have not cursed or lost my temper but on extremely rare occasions. Even when I smash my finger with a hammer or hurt myself in some way, I am not even cursing in my head any more. I have no doubt that my life is better because of these new habits.

I changed instantly and dramatically because I acknowledged the truth. These truths hit me so clearly that I was motivated to change my life to live according to them. When people change dramatically, when they do a U-Turn in life, it is usually because of something dramatic, and always toward something that they believe to be true.

Exploring the Resurrection

Jesus died. That is it. Even according to the Bible, Jesus says, "It is done," just before dying. When Jesus died on the cross and was buried, his disciples were lost and confused. After that, what happened? Is it possible to prove beyond a reasonable doubt that Jesus was resurrected or will Christians simply have to accept this central tenant of their faith on faith?

There are several obstacles to making the resurrection of Jesus believable, starting with the fact that it would have to be a miracle. If miracles are not possible, as David Hume contends, then it does not matter how implausible the alternatives are, they are more plausible than the miracle. If, however, you accept that "if God is possible miracles are possible," then at least we can begin.

So let's freeze time at the moment on Friday night when the disciples realized that Jesus was dead and he was not going to miraculously jump off of the cross. They went from being the triumphant entourage of the messiah to outlaws avoiding the law. They went from standing on the steady cornerstone to trying to balance on a rickety raft on raging waters not knowing where they were going.

> *³¹ Then Jesus told them, "This very night you will all fall away on account of me, for it is written:*
> *"'I will strike the shepherd,   and the sheep of the flock will be scattered.' - Matthew 26:31-32*
>
> *⁵⁶ But this has all taken place that the writings of the prophets might be fulfilled." Then all the disciples deserted him and fled. - Matthew 26:56*

74 Then he (Peter) began to call down curses, and he swore to them, "I do not know the man!" – Matthew 26:74

Fortunately, we do not have to start our search proving that Scripture is reliable. The Resurrection has been studied enough that even the most vehement skeptic accepts that

1. Jesus lived.
2. He claimed to be the Messiah. Matthew 26:63-64
3. He died on the cross. Matthew 27:50
4. He was buried. Matthew 27:57-61
5. The tomb was found empty. Matthew 28:5-6
6. The disciples claim to have seen Jesus again. Matthew 28:16-19

When we paused time on Friday night, there was no Christian Church. There were no plans for a Christian Church, no workers to build a Christian Church, and no message for a Christian Church. For all intents and purposes, the disciples were fired and told to go home. The public torture and crucifixion of Jesus would have been a humiliation to them as they contemplated going back to their pre-Jesus lives looking like fools for having followed him.

So what happened between Friday night and Sunday morning that changed the disciples into fearless teachers of the Word of God and the new covenant of salvation by grace through the Lord Jesus the Messiah?

We will look at the potential explanations for all three events and more.

There are six alternative explanations, besides accepting it as truth, for the empty tomb and the claim of post-death appearances of Jesus.

1. Stolen Body
2. Wrong Tomb
3. Not Jesus Who Died
4. Jesus Did not Die
5. Mass Hallucinations

6.   The Resurrection is a Myth

Can any of these explain the transformation of the disciples?

1.   The Stolen-Body Alternative

Could the disciples have stolen Jesus' body? This is what the Bible claims was the charge of the Jewish leaders when they found out that the tomb was found empty. The chances of the disciples overtaking the Roman guards posted at the tomb would have been unlikely as would the rolling back of the stone.

Attacking a Roman guard was a bad move for multiple reasons including that he would beat your butt and because if you were to somehow overtake him, you would become a fugitive of the Roman Empire. The Romans never pursued the disciples even though the disciples preached about inside knowledge of Jesus' disappearance/resurrection and were essentially incriminating themselves.

Does it make sense that the disciples would want to steal Jesus' body? It was well known that Jesus had claimed that he would die and rise three days later. If Jesus was going rise again, the disciples would have let him be. They had seen his miracles first hand for three years, including raising the dead.

If Jesus was not going to rise again, he was in a nice place. He had been buried in the tomb of a rich man instead of the mass grave he would have otherwise had. Why move him from there?

However, if the disciples had stolen the body, it would account for the empty tomb, but would it explain their transformation? If the disciples had stolen Jesus' body, would they then go out at great personal risk and begin preaching that he had risen? Does that make any sense?

In Acts chapter 4:18-20, Peter and John are put in jail by the rulers, the elders and the teachers of the law *"[18]commanded them not to speak or teach at all in the name of Jesus. [19] But Peter and John replied, "Which is right in God's eyes: to listen to you, or to him? You be the judges! [20] As for us, we cannot help speaking about what we have seen and heard."* In Acts 7:58, Stephen preached boldly to the leadership of Jerusalem, who *"[57] rushed at him, [58] dragged him out of the city and began to stone him. Meanwhile, the witnesses laid their coats at the feet of a young man named Saul."* Ultimately, the disciples were killed for their testimony about the risen Jesus.

Some will die for the truth, but no one will die for what they know is a lie. Do not miss the importance of this self-evident truth. Who would die for something they know is a lie? Saul a great prosecutor of the early Christian church had one of the most dramatic transformations in the Bible and he too paid with his life.

Building a False Religion on a Lie

This is a good place to add in some of the other verifiable evidence we have to see how it might play into the alternative explanation scenarios. You will be able to see the added difficulties with believing that the disciples knowingly created a false religion on a lie.

What the Disciples Gave Up

We may empathize with the disciples as they saw the opportunity to make their lives easier with regard to religion even if they justified it by a lie. If we had the chance to do the same today, we might say that services can't start before noon and that doughnuts are mandatory for every youth group gathering.

The disciples, however, lived in a society where their religion was the way of life for everyone, and it was no small thing to go against the Jewish leaders of the day. We can see what those leaders did to Jesus. Besides that, the disciples followed the Jewish law as a way of staying right with God. Any exit from the Jewish religion was at the risk of eternal damnation. But leave their religion was exactly what the disciples did. The book, *I Don't Have Enough Faith to be an Atheist* covers these in detail.

- They gave up animal sacrifice as the atonement for their sins.
- They gave up the hope in the written Law of Moses that was given to him by God to save the Jewish people.
- They gave up accepting that God was a singular being and instead accepted the trinity; God in three parts.
- They gave up honoring the Sabbath, which was a sacred tradition.
- They gave up looking for the Messiah that would be an earthly conquering king and instead accepted the suffering servant.

- They gave up the singular honor of being God's chosen people in order to teach salvation to the world.[cxxxi]

What They Burdened Themselves With

So if the disciples were really going to make a clean sweep of their lives and traditions for a lie, we may understand it if they chose a life of leisure and created a religion that would benefit them with money, power and sex. However, they seemed to make things harder on themselves. They rejected personal money and promiscuous sex, and the power they held seemed a burden that did not allow them to rest. They created a very challenging religion, completely contrary to human nature.

- Love your neighbor as yourself.
- Look at woman with lust and you have committed adultery.
- Divorce her and put her and the man she marries into a situation of committing adultery.
- Forgive your enemy. Pray for enemy. Turn the other cheek.
- Store up treasure in heaven.
- Be perfect just as Jesus was perfect.[cxxxii]

If the disciples knowingly created the Christian religion under false pretenses, they purposely gave up everything that they knew, created a difficult religion that gave no earthly payoff, and they did it all under the threat of imprisonment and death. Then finally, they were killed claiming that it was all true. Is it reasonable to believe that between Friday night and Sunday morning they decided to try to spread a lie?

2.   They Went to the Wrong Tomb Alternative

What if the women and then the men after them went to the wrong tomb? This would explain the empty tomb and their belief that whatever happened was not due to their own efforts.

It was early on Sunday morning and I am sure that the women were tired. They had only been to Jesus' tomb once and that was on Friday before the Sabbath so they may not have been familiar with the area. They may have taken a left instead of a right at the fig tree and ended up in the model tomb cul-de-sac instead of the recently occupied tombs. We know that the women raced back to Peter to bring him to the tomb, but what is the most reasonable expectation for what would happen next?

One way or another, the tomb would be identified as the wrong tomb. While running ahead of everyone to the tomb, Peter would probably go to the correct tomb to find it sealed. He would certainly be confused. But let's say that Peter made the same mistake that the women made and arrived at the empty tomb. At that point he exclaims, "Jesus is Risen!" He immediately goes back and starts running his mouth about the resurrected Jesus only to be embarrassed as the Jewish leaders open up the real tomb, pull Jesus' body out and put it on display at the Temple.

Furthermore, this scenario does not explain the claim by the disciples that they saw Jesus in physical form after the empty tomb. This scenario would have to incorporate massive lie as well.

3.   It Was Not Jesus Who Died on the Cross Alternative

This theory says that Jesus was not the person who was tortured and placed on the cross. Since Jesus did not really die, he was able to *appear* to the disciples and over 500 other witnesses after the tomb was found empty. Jesus' appearances would convince the disciples to truly believe in and claim a resurrected Jesus. At that point, the Christian Church is born, and it makes sense that the disciples would face danger and death for what they thought was the truth.

This scenario is troublesome to Christians on the surface, but the obstacles to how this set of events would have been arranged mount up pretty quickly. The substitute theory suggests that the Jews did not know what Jesus looked like and that the Romans made a huge mistake. It would mean that Jesus' mother and the disciples did not know what Jesus looked like or, that they knew it was not Jesus.

If a substitute died then the disciples would still have to steal the body and build a church on a lie. Or in a more bizarre twist, Jesus recruited others to steal the body of the substitute in order to maintain the belief of the disciples. This makes Jesus the ringmaster of a great deception and an egomaniac. In order to make his conspiracy work he would have had to leave the area for good and never come back. An egomaniac would never voluntarily give up the attention. If this is the Jesus of the substitute theory, it is much more likely that Jesus would have stayed and built the church on earth as the resurrected Messiah, and eventually die.

This theory would be like trying to arrange several puzzles into a single picture; an impossible mess.

4.   Jesus Was on the Cross but Did not Really Die Alternative

This is often called the swoon theory. The account of Jesus' torture and crucifixion are all accurate with one small exception, Jesus did not really die.

The Roman soldiers and everyone around him only thought that he had died. He was then placed in the tomb and the stone rolled across the door. When Jesus woke up from his near-death state he unwrapped his burial cloth and rolled back the incredibly heavy stone. He walked out unnoticed by the guards and made his way to appear to the disciples. ...I have to stop here.

It's silly to go on. It's like I am describing the person who was in a massive car accident in the morning, taken to the ER where he was rushed into surgery, which lasted several hours, and that evening he competed in and won the annual country-club tango contest with his wife.

Let's go through some of the problems with this theory. Imagine you are with the disciples hiding in a room. You are scared and uncertain, and you are discussing what you will do next when there is a weak knock on the door. You look at each other with concern. Then again, the knock. The youngest of you gets up and cracks open the door. He screams like a six-year-old girl and slams the door. He stands there panting with his shoulder against the door for a half a second until he realizes what he just saw. He throws the door open wide and Jesus falls into his arms unconscious from weakness and loss of blood. The disciples bring him in and do what?

a.   Immediately start to treat his wounds?

b.   Claim that he has risen from the dead as their Lord and Savior?

This theory assumes that you chose (b), or at least that you arrived at (b) after performing (a). From this point, Jesus either lives or he dies of his wounds. If he lived, where did he go, and if he died, why did the disciples claim that he was resurrected and ascended to heaven? Either way, the disciples were building Christianity on a lie.

5. The Disciples and Other Witnesses were Hallucinating Alternative

The Hallucination theory suggests that the disciples and others who saw Jesus during the six weeks between his death and supposed ascension to heaven were hallucinating. I do not believe that this holds much of a challenge to the biblical narrative since mass hallucinations do not happen. Even in the case where multiple people are hallucinating at the same time due to drugs or some other cause, they do not see the same things. These events, when reported do not include touching and talking and interacting.

The hallucinations would have to explain interactions with Jesus in multiple places, between multiple people, and sometimes with groups of people.

If we assume for a minute that everyone did hallucinate Jesus and were sincere in their belief, then it would explain their willingness to die for their belief. However, the Jewish leaders would have brought Jesus' body from the grave and posted it at the Temple. That would have been that.

6. The Story of Jesus Resurrection is a Myth Alternative

The myth theory says that Jesus may have lived, but that everything about his life and death gained supernatural scope as time went on. He went from a great moral teacher to a God as people added to the legend. In fact, they added to the Jesus Myth to other god myths that had existed prior to Jesus' life. This alternative says that there was no resurrection and the disciples never claimed such.

This theory might be good for a camp-fire story or among like-minded skeptics when no opposing view is proposed, but New Testament Scholars dismiss it as nonsense. Considering all of the evidence for the life and death of Jesus and the accepted events of the empty tomb and the claimed sightings, Jesus resurrection cannot be dismissed as a myth. The early dating of the Scripture soon after the death of Jesus, the early third-party writing concerning Jesus, and the beginning of the Christian Church simply make the myth theory unviable.

The Resurrection Event

The Resurrection is the defining event in Christianity. Paul says it as well as anyone can.

> *[14] And if Christ has not been raised, our preaching is useless and so is your faith. [15] More than that, we are then found to be false witnesses about God, for we have testified about God that he raised Christ from the dead. - 1 Corinthians 15:14-15*

The resurrection of Christ is either true or it's not. If the Biblical story of Jesus Resurrection is the best explanation for the empty tomb and the transformation of the lives of the disciples, then it demands a deeper look.

What was the purpose of Jesus' torture, death and new life? Our narrative has brought us from a purposeful creation of the Universe and of life to evil, mercy, miracles and eternity. The next chapter is the culmination of the decision-making process for you. If you can accept as reasonable the evidence that has brought you this far, then Salvation is a breath away…but is it true?

Implications of Each Conclusion
Believing that the resurrection did not occur leaves you trying to explain the established facts in some alternative manner.

If you accept that Jesus Christ was resurrected and ascended into Heaven, then you should explore why his death, burial, resurrection and ascension were necessary.

Answer the Assessment questions from the beginning of the chapter again

Characteristics of the Resurrector
- All Powerful
- Purposeful
- Loving

Deliverables
- Even the most vehement skeptic accepts that
    - Jesus lived.
    - He claimed to be the Messiah. Matthew 26:63-64
    - He died on the cross. Matthew 27:50
    - He was buried. Matthew 27:57-61
    - The tomb was found empty. Matthew 28:5-6
    - The disciples claim to have seen Jesus again. Matthew 28:16-19
- Jesus Body was never produced by skeptics.
- In earthly terms the disciples gave up everything and gained nothing but trouble.
- The disciples went from scattered and scared to bold and courageous in building the church.
- The disciples were killed for maintaining their testimony about Jesus as the Messiah was true.
- None of the alternative explanations adequately explain the established facts.

CHAPTER 14

Salvation

Is Salvation Necessary or Logical?

Possible Conclusions

1. No. Salvation is not necessary or logical. The false salvation agenda is the result of people's need to have some hope for an afterlife.
2. Yes. Salvation is necessary and logical. Salvation through Christ Jesus is the only path to heaven. Salvation through Christ Jesus is the first decision of a life submitted to God.

Assessment

Question	Before Reading	After Reading
Every religion provides a path to heaven.	Y/T - N/F	Y/T - N/F
It is possible to do enough good work to get to heaven	Y/T - N/F	Y/T - N/F
The need or method of eternal salvation cannot be reasonably proven.	Y/T - N/F	Y/T - N/F
Christianity is a crutch for those who want to avoid the hard questions of life.	Y/T - N/F	Y/T - N/F
Christians just want to have comfort believing that they are going to go to heaven.	Y/T - N/F	Y/T - N/F
Hypocrisy is saying/believing one thing and doing another.	Y/T - N/F	Y/T - N/F

Salvation Introduction

Anyone saying that salvation is not a provable concept did not know me before I was saved. But then, no one knew who I really was before I was saved. On the outside I was like most everyone else – normal. I was selfless in many ways. I loved my family, and I legitimately cared for and served the soldiers in my units. I was hard working and I believe easy to get along with. But on the inside I was uncertain and selfish.

I was raised agnostic, churchless, without a care about eternity one way or the other and yet, without prompting, time and again I wondered about God. I was pessimistic about the future of our country and the world to the point of not desiring to bring children into the world. I was constantly worried about my career and my ability to create a secure financial future. I worried a lot. I was cynical, introverted and judgmental and yet I still believed that I was a good person. I walked around with a very high self-image.

I was lost and I did not even know it. When I took enough time to think about the possibility of the existence of God, the amount of ambiguity and lack of clarity made me quickly abandon the exercise. But the nagging feeling that I was missing something always remained.

My beliefs about God were built from bits and pieces I inadvertently picked up throughout my life. There was no structure, no guidance and no plan to my education. I heard things from friends and listened to National Geographic and NOVA deal with God-level issues without the mention of God. I heard about silly restrictive Christian traditions like the *Wedding Song* being banned as a pagan song. I took on the view that Christianity demanded what I believed were unreasonable restrictions on my pursuit of personal happiness. My impression of Christianity was not based on any kind of thoughtful inquiry. The Bible provides the simple logic for my situation.

> *"[14] How, then, can they call on the one they have not believed in? And how can they believe in the one of whom they have not heard? And how can they hear without someone preaching to them?"* [cxxxiii]

So I remained restless. As Augustine explains, "You have made us for yourselves, Oh Lord, and our hearts are restless until they find rest in you."[cxxxiv]

Even after the time that I realized that I was a horrible judge of my own character and knew that I was supposed to be a Christian, I kept it to myself. I knew where I had to be, but I was not ready to give up the activities in my life that I enjoyed, but which I knew were against Christian beliefs. I was ready to jump behind the Christian wall if I was shot at, but until then, I would enjoy the habits I knew I would soon have to give up. I started reading the Bible a little bit and even began attending a Bible study with a group of couples.

The Bible study was the weirdest thing in the world. The people were really nice, and we sat around the table and sang songs while one of the guys played an acoustic guitar. The experience should have felt fake and plastic, but it didn't. There was something to the environment and the people that encouraged me and I wanted more.

As my faith built and I got married to my wife Natasha, we started our faith journey together. I still did not read the Bible much, but I was sure proud of myself when I did. It was hard to take the time to read the Bible when I was so busy with my career.

Once I believed that Jesus died for my sins, I never doubted that I was in line with the truth. Even now, I do not know all of the facts and I do not have absolute knowledge about Christ's sacrifice or God's plan, but the Holy Spirit has made me a new creation. I have learned the joy of forgiving others and myself. I have learned how to have peace through difficult circumstances. Sadly, I've had too much practice. I have worked to treat my earthly possessions as God's possessions and I have attempted to love others as I love myself. None of that was or is easy, however, unlike my previous self, I am at peace. I am confident in my beliefs. I am in the Bible every day now and aggressively studying God's word and world, and the evidence for His existence.

I have three children, which I would not have had and which are pure joy to me through the good and bad. I have been married for 25 years to a woman with whom I share everything including the commitment to do the hard work to make our marriage honoring to God.

My decision to accept the free gift of salvation from God turned my life. When the nagging for that something missing was filled with Christ, the nagging went away.

Exploring Salvation

Why are we talking about salvation as an apologetic topic? A skeptic might say that salvation, the need to be forgiven of our sins, is a purely religious topic. It belongs in discussions alongside reincarnation, the Universal consciousness and nothingness. The fact is that Salvation is the ultimate apologetic subject. The work that you have done through this book has all been to determine if Salvation is a true necessity or a false belief.

Salvation is an apologetic subject because it is one of the possible explanations that unify the rest of the subjects. What is the most reasonable next step in the progression of evidence that we have looked at? The implications of choosing to believe in God or choosing to believe in the reliability of Scripture is that you have an obligation to seek the purpose that God has for you. What can best bring together all of the decisions that you have made to this point? Should you believe that God's plan is to reconcile you to him by offering you the ability to be sinless in his judgement or is there a better explanation for the evidence we have explored? We started on a journey for Truth and it has naturally brought us to the wrapping up of a worldview in a way that makes sense.

Our journey has allowed us to evaluate and decide our position on several subjects.

1. If God created this Universe and formed it to allow for life, and then He created all life, does it make sense that he did it for a purpose?
2. If Humans carry with them an innate moral standard and justly hate evil and suffering, then is there a reason for that sense?
3. If Scriptures were written by eye witnesses and brought accurately to today, should we believe what they say and act accordingly?
4. If Hell and miracles are possible and compatible with an all loving, all powerful God, then do they have a purpose?
5. If fulfilled prophecy laces Scripture together in hundreds of ways, then should we believe what it forecasts for the future?
6. If Jesus was killed on the cross and resurrected, then could he have done it for the Salvation of mankind as Scriptures foretold?

Or is there a better explanation?

> *"If you believe what you like in the gospels, and reject what you do not like, it is not the gospel you believe, but yourself." – Saint Augustine*

If you believe that there is a better explanation for the body of evidence that you have explored, then what might it be? You have freed yourself from the commitment to God and his Word, and you are free to imagine for yourself whatever you like.

Unification

It is interesting that scientists have been on the hunt for the elusive, unifying Theory of Everything (ToE). The ToE "is a hypothetical single, all-encompassing, coherent theoretical framework of physics that fully explains and links together all physical aspects of the universe." [cxxxv] The laws of physics are broken into two parts, those laws that govern sub-atomic matter and those which govern everything else. As you shrink from a marble to an atom, you have to change physics busses. These two sets of laws are like feuding brothers and you can't have them both over to the house at the same time otherwise dishes will get broken. Needless to say, scientists are trying desperately to figure out how to reconcile these two laws.

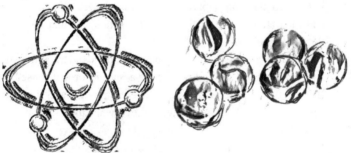

As individuals, we want unity too. We want our decisions about God and Creation and Jesus to make sense together, even if we reject it all. Even at this point in our progress, you may still have doubts. That is normal, but do you have enough information to make a decision on the subject of ultimate purpose?

History from the Beginning of Time
-   Creation of the Universe
-   Creation of Adam and Eve in the Garden of Eden

-   Adam and Eve in relationship with God
-   Adam and Eve choose to sin
-   Man separated from relationship with God by their sin.
-   Man now suffers physical death and judgement.
-   Man gets really bad and God wipes them out with the worldwide flood.
-   Man populates the earth, and Jacob has 12 sons. The Nation of Israel is born.
-   Laws are given to the nation of Israel in order to continually reconcile them with God.
-   A Messiah who will rescue the Jews and save all nations is prophesized from the beginning.
-   Jesus fulfills prophecies by being born at the right time, in the right place, in the right family.
-   Jesus fulfills prophecies by growing up to claim the right things, do the right things, and present himself as the messiah on the right day.
-   Jesus claims to take mans' punishment on himself in death and fulfills prophecy by rising from the dead.
-   Man is reconciled to God again through belief that Jesus died for our sins.

- Jesus gives the Great Commission. *"¹⁹ Therefore go and make disciples of all nations, baptizing them in the name of the Father and of the Son and of the Holy Spirit, ²⁰ and teaching them to obey everything I have commanded you.'" – Matthew 28:19-20*
- Disciples and eye witnesses write books about their experiences and what Jesus taught them.
- The church makes thousands of accurate copies of these books and passes them to each generation.
- Those books are called Scripture, The Bible.

Truth in Jesus

The evidence for each of the essential steps of this history have been represented in this book. In my opinion, that evidence adds up to support the conclusion that Jesus died on the cross for you. But what about all of those other great religions? There are billions of Muslims and Hindus, hundreds of millions of Buddhists and millions of Mormons. Why can't they all be right?

Bottom Line. Jesus claimed to be the only path to God.

"Jesus answered, "I am the way and the truth and the life. No one comes to the Father except through me" – John 14:6

and you cannot achieve salvation by doing good things.

"For it is by grace you have been saved, through faith—and this is not from yourselves, it is the gift of God— not by works, so that no one can boast. – Ephesians 2:8-9

- Truth: Jesus either died on the cross for your sins or he did not.
- Truth: Jesus is the only way to God or he is not.

If you are satisfied the evidence presented throughout this book is strong enough for you to choose Jesus, then no matter how much it might hurt to realize, the other religions are choosing to reject Christ and will end up in Hell. If you are confident that you hold the truth in Jesus, and you yearn badly enough to save the rest of the world, then do it. With Jesus you have the ability to save them for eternity. Without Jesus, you may be able to feed some and heal some, but it will be for no ultimate purpose.

The Hard Choice

Accepting Jesus is not the easier path as some skeptics would suggest. It is not a crutch to rest on because of a weak intellect or selfish desire to avoid Hell or achieve Heaven. Christianity is a demanding religion that expects you to learn how to forgive others no matter what they have done to you because God first forgave you. Christianity expects you to have peace through adversity because your trust is in God's plan. You are expected to treat your earthly possessions as temporary and use them to advance his Kingdom and to save other people. Christianity expects you to recognize truth and to stand on truth even when it is unpopular. Christianity expects you to love others as you love yourself. Christianity expects you to repent and to forgive yourself for the mistakes you have made because you are not guilty and should not live that way.

This hard choice demanded by the Bible is sometimes criticized as restrictive to freedom. Could it be that those restrictions are for our own good? Paul says, *"I have the right to do anything,"* ...—*but not everything is beneficial. "I have the right to do anything"—but not everything is constructive."*[cxxxvi] When we are acting under our own freedom, we behave in ways that shackle us with regrets, guilt, stress, anxiety, and negative consequences. That's not true freedom. When we accept that God knows better, we put ourselves into submission to guidance that we do not fully understand in order to have the greater freedom of peace, contentment and freedom from guilt.

- What are the consequences of not speaking in anger?
- What are the consequences of forgiving?

- What are the consequences of not taking drugs?
- What are the consequences of not cheating on your spouse?
- What are the consequences of not having pre-marital sex?
- What are the consequences of not committing a crime?
- What are the consequences of not having an abortion?
- What are the consequences of obeying your parents?

No matter your circumstances or behavior in the past there is hope – right now – in Jesus Christ. The Bible reveals God's plan for the reconciliation of the world to himself through the sacrifice of Jesus Christ. It is a plan that includes you. *"For all have sinned and fall short of the glory of God, and all are justified freely by his grace through the redemption that came by Christ Jesus."*[cxxxvii] Jesus has already paid the penalty for your sins. There are earthly consequences to our behaviors, but there is eternal life freely available to those who accept Jesus Christ as their savior.

God's expectations set you up against the world. You may already be struggling with how to tell your friends that you are a Christian, or how to treat homosexuals, or how to forgive someone who has hurt you so badly. You may struggle with the intolerance of believing that other religions will go to Hell or how you can have peace through the current difficulties in your life.

If Jesus died on the cross for your sins so you can someday stand before God innocent of your sins, then weigh that with the discomfort you may feel at making or strengthening your commitment to Christ.

Replacing Hypocrisy with Hypocrisy
I said at the beginning of this book that many Christians are not at peace within themselves because of the conflict between their intellect and their faith. Their intellect tells them that scientific evidence points away from the existence of God while their faith says that God loves them. This struggle produces people who are meek and unsure. This self-perceived hypocrisy keeps them from spreading the gospel. These Christians carry around a sense of dishonesty that they do not know how to shake.

Before reading this book you may have felt that there was no evidence for Christianity, now however, even if you do not accept the conclusions, you know differently. If your struggle is no longer an intellectual one, it is a motivational one. You may now have to come to grips with the belief that Christianity is true because of the evidence, and what that belief demands of your behaviors. You risk becoming a hypocrite for the exact opposite reason as when you started this book.

In his book, *Reasonable Faith*, William Lane Craig paraphrases Alvin Plantiga, who observes how "to move someone from knowledge to ignorance by presenting him with a valid argument based on premises he knows to be true for a conclusion he does not want to accept! No better illustration of this can be given than the natural man's refusing to believe in God or Christ at the expense of adopting some outlandish hypothesis which he ought to know is false."[cxxxviii]

Some people simply do not like Christianity and will not accept it as true for any reason, but would you want to be on the opposite side of the evidence I exposed in this book? Can you imagine sitting at a coffee shop insisting that the Universe popped into existence out of nothing uncaused, or how you are pretty certain that Jesus only seemed to die on the cross? These conversations will happen.

You must choose one way or the other. Christ died in order to take the punishment due to you, or he did not. The decisions you have made up to this point are not simply academic in nature. They have all been in support of or opposed to the necessity of your personal salvation.

I welcome your testimony. Please take a moment to go to the website at www.bracebarber.com/testimony to let me know if this book has helped you make a decision for Christ or strengthened your faith. If you are still struggling with doubts, I invite you to write to me directly.

Implications of Each Conclusion

Believing that Salvation is not necessary or logical is a self-fulfilling request. If you reject the claim that Jesus took your sins to the cross in order to give you innocence at the day of judgement, then he hasn't. The responsibility for that decision rests on you. During this life you are free to pursue whatever purpose you create for yourself.

Believing that Salvation is necessary, and by accepting that Jesus took your sins to the cross in order to give you innocence at the day of judgement, then he has. You are innocent. You should not use your future freedom in eternity to purposely add to the sin that Jesus bore, but rather respond in thankfulness at the opportunity to receive forgiveness. You should serve God in response to his grace.

> Answer the Assessment questions from the beginning of the chapter again

Characteristics of the Salvation Giver
- All Loving
- Just
- Merciful
- Eternal
- Purposeful

Deliverables
- The best explanation for the evidence we have is that God is working to reconcile his people to him.
- There is a purpose in every biblical act and component.
- If Jesus is the only way to God, then all religions that add to or take away from this belief are false.
- Christianity is not a crutch, rather it is a yoke that demands self-control in order to present a life filled with forgiveness, peace, service, generosity, love and innocence.
- The pursuit of our physical pleasure and emotional desires can be an obstacle to accepting the evidence for Christ.

Conclusion

Exploring Decisions

You have made 14 decisions as you have come through this book. Even if you believe that you have not made a decision, you have. I remember my first solo parachute jump out of a helicopter. I jumped out into the incredible wind and noise. I was taking in the view farmland and forest below me, and the reality of my experience as I sped towards my collision with earth.

I never hesitated to pull the ripcord. I never wondered whether or not it was going to work. I was not a skeptic about whether or not my parachute would work. Parachutes did not work 100% of the time, but I did not question the overwhelming evidence that my parachute would most likely open when I pulled the cord.  Many people, especially youth, do not realize that they are falling and that there is a fatal stop awaiting them. Many people will use the excuse that they do not have 100% proof of God or Jesus and therefore they are justified on sitting on the sideline until they do. …You are still falling and gravity does not slow down for skeptics.

It would be silly to say that I do not have an agenda or perspective with this book. I want to encourage you to make a choice for your personal salvation in Jesus Christ. However, I know for a fact that I can't talk you into Christianity, force you to convert, or overcome your doubts and concerns 100%. What I can try to do is reduce the gap that must be filled by faith. Every skeptic and atheist has a gap of faith between where they are now and becoming a Christian. The gap for an atheist may be 100%, whereas the gap for someone raised in a Christian home may be 20%.

For Christians Only

Even if you have chosen for God and Scripture and Jesus right down the line, your journey is just beginning. Fortunately, you are now armed with more ammunition than you need to boldly defend the Word of God and his plan for Salvation among your friends and family. You have become part of a small but growing group of Christians who are capable of expanding Christianity instead of hoping that the Christian faith in America does not dwindle to nothing in your lifetime.

More good news, this book provides a very high-level of evidence in support of your Christian faith. There are wonderful, expansive sources of education for whatever dimension of apologetics you are interested in. You should know now that the balance of evidence between Christianity and Agnosticism and Atheism is not even close. Christians do not have to close their eyes to scientific, historic and philosophical evidence; the skeptics do. They have to ignore the obvious conclusions that every area of inquiry is producing in support of the Christian claims of Creation, Life, Scripture and Salvation. Your ammo never runs out. Use it to save.

Battle

This is not a battle to kill, but a battle to save your enemy, and you are on the front lines. From high-school through the age of 22 is typically the most target-rich environment. You are experiencing the first freedoms from your parents and exploring what it means to be a responsible adult. You are testing the beliefs that were given to you by your parents and Church to determine if they are the same ones you want to carry into your adult years. You are being bombarded with the *education* of the world, filled with every anti-God, anti-Christian interpretation possible. To make matters worse, you have the opportunity and desire to begin experiencing the sensual pleasures of life.

The battle will not be easy and you will not be perfect, but everyone around you, including those raised in agnostic, atheistic and other types of homes is searching for truth as well. Get this! When you are in the conversations regarding world views and philosophy and truth that naturally happen in these age groups, you are bringing hard evidence and hope that none of them will have. You ca	make a difference in the eternities of countless people.

In these environments is where the Christian Church in America begins to grow again. Just the Evangelical Christian Church in America has been losing about .13% every year and now is only 25.4% of the Adult US population. The loss may not seem like much, and we still have plenty of people, but if the trend stays the same over the next 40 years, we will have lost over 18 million Evangelical followers of Christ, not including losses from other denominations dedicated to following Christ. If however, we add only .07% every year the Christian church will grow by 9 million souls in the same time period![cxxxix]

> *"so is my word that goes out from my mouth: It will*
> *not return to me empty, but will accomplish what I*
> *desire and achieve the purpose for which I sent it." –*
> *Isaiah 55:11*

Other Books and Programs by Brace

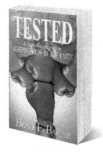

TESTED: A New Strategy for Keeping Kids in the Faith. Brace demolishes the belief that the Christian Church can't win the battle for our kids against 'science' and the public school system. In fact, he goes so far as to say that Christianity dominates easily in every area of study, and then he gives you a step-by-step method for effectively arming your kids with this powerful knowledge. Skeptical? Great. Reach out to Brace on Facebook.

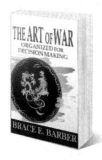

The Art of War Organized for Decision Making. A Must Have Resource for Every Art of War Enthusiast. Strategic planning with The Art of War is now possible. The effective application of Sun Tzu's Art of War was a guessing game prior to this organization of the book. Brace Barber discarded proverbs meaningless to modern society in order to focus the reader, eliminate distraction and allow for clear strategic thinking. He then reorganized the Art of War in line with accepted strategic categories necessary for systematically analyzing a problem and developing a highly stable course of action. This book is your key to an advanced strategic IQ.

Ranger School, No Excuse Leadership. Experience the inspiring true stories of Army Rangers going through the leadership crucible of Army Ranger School. Great for any reader looking for adventure and perspective in these tough times. The challenge, the pain and the leadership value of U. S. Army Ranger School have been squeezed into the pages of this book. Experience the first book to illuminate the best leadership school in the U.S. Army; Ranger School. Ranger School puts you at ground level and drives home leadership principles through impactful first-person stories.

Create the Know. I personally work with only one executive or owner at a time in an exclusive venue over 48-hours in order to create a highly stable, highly strategic course of action for a selected complex and thorny mission. Within minutes of starting the Full Spectrum Decision Making Process, I get clients shedding the weight of conflicting priorities and we begin tearing into the meat of their mission. By the end of the two days, they have a roughed out, highly stable course of action planned and ready for the inclusion of other stakeholders.

[i] Letter to a Christian Nation By Sam Harris, Knopf, September 19, 2006
[ii] I reversed the verse. 25 then 24.
[iii] I Do not Have Enough Faith to be an Atheist, by Norman L. Geisler and Frank Turek. Pg 37-38, 2004 Crossway
[iv] http://www.reasonablefaith.org/argument-from-contingency
[v] 10^{80} atoms in the Universe. https://www.thoughtco.com/number-of-atoms-in-the-universe-603795#:~:text=The%20universe%20is%20vast.%20Scientists%20estimate%20there%20are,value%20and%20not%20just%20some%20random%2C%20made-up%20number.
[vi] Harry Cliff, Ted Talk, Have we reached the end of Physics? http://www.ted.com/talks/harry_cliff_have_we_reached_the_end_of_physics
[vii] George Gamow and Albert Einstein: Did Einstein say the cosmological constant was the "biggest blunder" he ever made in his life? Galina Weinstein, October 3, 2013
[viii] G. Lemaître (April 1927). "Un Univers homogène de masse constante et de rayon croissant rendant compte de la vitesse radiale des nébuleuses extra-galactiques". Annales de la Société Scientifique de Bruxelles (in French) 47: 49. Bibcode:1927ASSB...47...49L.
[ix] In the Beginning Was the Beginning. By Jacqueline Mitchell http://now.tufts.edu/articles/beginning-was-beginning. May 29, 2012
[x] https://www.amazon.com/Universe-Nothing-There-Something-Rather/dp/1451624468
[xi] Has Physics Made Philosophy and Religion Obsolete? By Ross Anderson, April 23, 2012. The Atlantic. http://www.theatlantic.com/technology/archive/2012/04/has-physics-made-philosophy-and-religion-obsolete/256203/
[xii] VIDEO: 2016 Isaac Asimov Memorial Debate: Is the Universe a Simulation? https://www.youtube.com/watch?v=wgSZA3NPpBs
[xiii] Signature in the Cell: DNA and the Evidence for Intelligent Design https://www.amazon.com/Signature-Cell-Evidence-Intelligent-Design/dp/0061472794/ref=sr_1_2?dchild=1&hvadid=78546492259369&hvbmt=bp&hvdev=c&hvqmt=p&keywords=signature+in+the+cell&qid=1599780742&sr=8-2&tag=mh0b-20
[xiv] http://espn.go.com/nba/statistics/player/_/stat/free-throws/sort/freeThrowPct
[xv] http://82games.com/locations.htm
[xvi] http://www.reasonablefaith.org/transcript-fine-tuning-argument
[xvii] Powerball Drawing Detail, Drawing Date: Wednesday, January 13, 2016 https://www.usamega.com/powerball-drawing.asp?d=1/13/2016
[xviii] Powerball Winning Numbers Wednesday, Jan. 13, 2016 By Todd Richissin http://patch.com/texas/downtownaustin/what-time-tonights-15-billion-powerball-drawing-texas
[xix] http://www.npr.org/sections/krulwich/2012/09/17/161096233/which-is-greater-the-number-of-sand-grains-on-earth-or-stars-in-the-sky 7.5 x 1018 grains of sand
[xx] Heeren, F. 1995. Show Me God. Wheeling, IL, Searchlight Publications, p. 200. http://www.godandscience.org/apologetics/quotes.html#n06
[xxi] http://www.seti.org/node/61
[xxii] RTB Design Compendium (2009) By Dr. Hugh Ross November 17, 2010 http://www.reasons.org/articles/rtb-design-compendium-2009
[xxiii] Reasonable Faith, Christian Truth and Apologetics, Third Edition, William Lane Craig, Crossway Publishing, 2008, Pg159
[xxiv] On Guard, Defending Your Faith with Reason and Precision By William Lane Craig,

David C. Cook Publishing, 2010 Pg 109

[xxv] Reasonable Faith, Christian Truth and Apologetics, Third Edition, William Lane Craig, Crossway Publishing, 2008, Pg158

[xxvi] Reasonable Faith, Christian Truth and Apologetics, Third Edition, William Lane Craig, Crossway Publishing, 2008, Pg158

[xxvii] Fred Hoyle, "The Universe: Past and Present Reflections." Engineering and Science, November, 1981. pp. 8–12

[xxviii] Have We Reached the End of Physics? December 2015 Harry Cliff, Science Museum Fellow at University of Cambridge. Conducting research into matter-antimatter asymmetry as part of the LHCb collaboration at CERN

[xxix] Lawrence M. Krauss, A Universe from Nothing: Why There Is Something Rather Than Nothing, January 10, 2012 Atria Books

[xxx] Alternative Definition for Artificial Intelligence: Artificial intelligence could jokingly be called that which passes itself off as true intelligence, but which is really undeniable ignorance dressed up with haughty academic language and the consensus of like-minded people.

[xxxi] Bionumbers. The Database of Useful Biological Numbers http://bionumbers.hms.harvard.edu/bionumber.aspx?&id=100017&ver=6

[xxxii] Bionumbers. The Database of Useful Biological Numbers http://bionumbers.hms.harvard.edu/bionumber.aspx?&id=107699&ver=2&trm=differe nt%20types%20of%20proteins%20in%20e.coli

[xxxiii] In the Beginning, Compelling Evidence for Creation and the Flood by Walt Brown, Ph.D 2015

[xxxiv] Carl Sagan, The Dragons of Eden (New York: Random House, 1977), p. 25.

[xxxv] Has Physics Made Philosophy and Religion Obsolete? Ross Andersen, Apr 23, 2012

[xxxvi] The Origin of Species, By Charles Darwin. Chapter 6 - Difficulties on Theory

[xxxvii] Cambrian Explosion, Paleobiology, http://www.fossilmuseum.net/Paleobiology/CambrianExplosion.htm

[xxxviii] Darwin's Dilemma, Stephen Meyer, Paul Nelson, Lad Allen. DVD Illustra Media Oct 29, 2010

[xxxix] River out of Eden, by Richard Dawkins Basic Books, 1995 p.83

[xl] The Origin of Species, By Charles Darwin

[xli] In the Beginning, Compelling Evidence for Creation and the Flood by Walt Brown, Ph.D 2015 Pg 3

[xlii] Darwin's Dilemma, Stephen Meyer, Paul Nelson, Lad Allen. DVD Illustra Media Oct 29, 2010

[xliii] Darwin's Dilemma, Stephen Meyer, Paul Nelson, Lad Allen. DVD Illustra Media Oct 29, 2010

[xliv] Darwin's Black Box: The Biochemical Challenge to Evolution by Michael J. Behe Free Press, August 2, 1996

[xlv] The Origin of Species, By Charles Darwin

[xlvi] Is Intelligent Design Theory Science? http://www.str.org/articles/is-intelligent-design-theory-science#.Vx-stY-cHIU by J. Warner Wallace January 1, 2013

[xlvii] Intelligent Design on Trial. Science is "Exhibit A" in a landmark trial on the teaching of evolution. Aired November 13, 2007 on PBS

[xlviii] Dawkins, R., The Blind Watchmaker, W.W. Norton & Company, New York, USA, p. 1, 1986.

[xlix] God Is Not Great: How Religion Poisons Everything, By Christopher Hitchens, Twelve Books, May 1, 2007

[l] The God Delusion By Richard Dawkins, Houghton Mifflin Co, October 18th 2006

li The Moral Landscape, How Science can Determine Human Values, By Sam Harris, Free Press, October 2010

lii Holy Bible, New International Version®, NIV® Copyright ©1973, 1978, 1984, 2011 by Biblica, Inc.

liii Holy Bible, New International Version®, NIV® Copyright ©1973, 1978, 1984, 2011 by Biblica, Inc.

liv Holy Bible, New International Version®, NIV® Copyright ©1973, 1978, 1984, 2011 by Biblica, Inc.

lv Navigating Sam Harris' The Moral Landscape by William Lane Craig, Enrichment Journal, Fall 2012

lvi The Selfish Gene By Richard Dawkins, Oxford University Press, May 25th 2006

lvii SS Andrea Doria, From Wikipedia, the free encyclopedia

lviii Nigeria's Stolen Girls: Inside Boko Haram Territory Where Children Are Forced to Become Suicide Bombers: Reporter's Notebook by Juju Chang, Apr 27, 2016,

lix Nigeria's Stolen Girls: Inside Boko Haram Territory Where Children Are Forced to Become Suicide Bombers: Reporter's Notebook by Juju Chang, Apr 27, 2016,

lx Amish School Shooting http://lancasterpa.com/amish/amish-school-shooting/ October 2nd, 2006

lxi Stephen Fry, On God the Meaning of Life RTE One

lxii North Korea: Celebration reinforces Kim dynasty's iron grip on power, By Tim Schwarz, CNN, October 9, 2015

lxiii North Korea: Human rights concerns, Amnesty International Australia

lxiv Stephen Fry, On God the Meaning of Life RTE One

lxv From Amazon.com introduction to Forged: Writing in the Name of God--Why the Bible's Authors Are Not Who We Think They Are By Bart D. Ehrman

lxvi Writing in the Name of God--Why the Bible's Authors Are Not Who We Think They Are By Bart D. Ehrman

lxvii The Gospel according to Bart by Daniel B. Wallace April 24, 2006

lxviii Cold-Case Christianity, A Homicide Detective Investigates the Claims of the Gospels, by J. Warner Wallace. David C. Cook, 2013 Pg. 169

lxix I Do not Have Enough Faith to be an Atheist, by Norman L. Geisler and Frank Turek. Pg 225, 2004 Crossway

lxx I Do not Have Enough Faith to be an Atheist, by Norman L. Geisler and Frank Turek. Pg 227, 2004 Crossway

lxxi I Do not Have Enough Faith to be an Atheist, by Norman L. Geisler and Frank Turek. Pg 227, 2004 Crossway

lxxii William Lane Craig speaks at Gracepoint Berkeley Church on The Work of Bart Ehrman, Gracepoint Berkeley Church, Berkeley, California, April 17, 2010

lxxiii Listerine http://www.listerine.com/

lxxiv Bart Ehrman, Misquoting Jesus, New York: Harper San Francisco, 2005, Pg 252-3

lxxv Luke 4:16-21

lxxvi http://dss.collections.imj.org.il/isaiah

lxxvii Can We Construct The Entire New Testament From the Writings of the Church Fathers? By J. Warner Wallace, January 10, 2013

lxxviii 10 Ignored Warnings That Were Tragically Deadly by Elizabeth S. Anderson May 12, 2016 http://listverse.com/2016/05/12/10-ignored-warnings-that-turned-deadly/

lxxix In The Beginning. Pg 119.

lxxx In The Beginning. Pg 206.

lxxxi In The Beginning. Pg 119

lxxxii In The Beginning. Pg 121.

[lxxxiii] The World's a Graveyard; Flood Evidence Number Two by Dr. Andrew A. Snelling on February 12, 2008

[lxxxiv] In The Beginning. Pg 158

[lxxxv] http://pubs.usgs.gov/publications/text/fire.html

[lxxxvi] In The Beginning. Pg 171

[lxxxvii] In The Beginning. Pg 170

[lxxxviii] In The Beginning. Pg 168

[lxxxix] Earthquakes and the Earth's Rotation, By John Maddox, Nature, March, 3 1988

[xc] Japan Quake May Have Shortened Earth Days, Moved Axis By Alan Buis, Jet Propulsion Laboratory March 14, 2011

[xci] In The Beginning. Pg 114

[xcii] In The Beginning. Pg 171

[xciii] Wayne Ranney, Carving the Grand Canyon: Evidence, Theories, and Mystery (Grand Canyon, Arizona: Grand Canyon Association, 2005), back cover.

[xciv] In The Beginning. Pg 211

[xcv] In The Beginning. Pg 217

[xcvi] In The Beginning. Pg 214

[xcvii] In The Beginning. Pg 214 Figure 118

[xcviii] In The Beginning. Pg 220-221

[xcix] In The Beginning. Pg 237 Figure 137

[c] The National Registry of Exonerations https://www.law.umich.edu/special/exoneration/Pages/casedetail.aspx?caseid=4640

[ci] http://www.murderpedia.org/male.B/b1/bundy-ted-victims.htm

[cii] Huie, William Bradford (January 1956). "The Shocking Story of Approved Killing in Mississippi". Look Magazine. Retrieved October 2010.

[ciii] Whitfield, Stephen (1991). A Death in the Delta: The story of Emmett Till, JHU Press. ISBN 978-0-8018-4326-6

[civ] Hebrews 4:12-13

[cv] Matthew 13:42

[cvi] Revelation 14:10

[cvii] John 14:6

[cviii] Hebrews 9:14-16

[cix] US Army Captain Finell, English 101 Professor 1983

[cx] Can the Existence and Nature of Hell be Defended? By J. Warner Wallace July 1, 2014

[cxi] Hebrews 10:28-29 Note: Anyone who rejected the law of Moses died without mercy on the testimony of two or three witnesses.
How much more severely do you think someone deserves to be punished who has trampled the Son of God underfoot, who has treated as an unholy thing the blood of the covenant that sanctified them, and who has insulted the Spirit of grace?

[cxii] Hebrews 9:26-28

[cxiii] An Inconvenient Review: After 10 Years Al Gore's Film Is Still Alarmingly Inaccurate, By Michael Batasch, May 3, 2016

[cxiv] Septuagint and Reliability, Septuagint.net

[cxv] Dead Sea Scrolls, All About Archaeology, allaboutarchaeology.org

[cxvi] I compressed some of the text for clarity of reading. No meaning was changed.

[cxvii] Luke 4:21

[cxviii] Revelation 19:14

[cxix] The Book "The Coming Prince," By Sir Robert Anderson, walks through the calendars as they existed from 445 BC through 32 AD to identify the exact dates and years that the prophesized events occurred. It is a free book available from Gutenberg Press.

[cxx] The Coming Prince, By Sir Robert Anderson 1894

[cxxi] The Precision of Prophecy, Daniels 70 Weeks, By Chuck Missler

[cxxii] Has Physics Made Philosophy and Religion Obsolete? By Ross Anderson, April 23, 2012. The Atlantic.

[cxxiii] 2016 Isaac Asimov Memorial Debate: Is the Universe a Simulation? April 2016 hosted by Neil deGrasse Tyson at the American Museum of Natural History

[cxxiv] River out of Eden, by Richard Dawkins Basic Books, 1995

[cxxv] The Problem of Miracles: A Historical and Philosophical Perspective by William Lane Craig

[cxxvi] The Problem of Miracles: A Historical and Philosophical Perspective by William Lane Craig

[cxxvii] Samuel Clarke, *A Discourse concerning the Unchangeable Obligations of Natural Religion and the Truth and Certainty of the Christian Revelation* (London: W. Botham, 1706)

[cxxviii] J. Alph. Turretin, *Traité de la vérité de la religion chrétienne,* 2nd ed., 7 vols., trans. J. Vernet (Genéve: Henri-Albert Gosse, 1745-55)

[cxxix] How to Win Friends and Influence People, by Dale Carnegie, Simon and Schuster, 1936

[cxxx] 7 Habits of Highly Successful People, by Steven R. Covey, Simon and Schuster, 1989. The image was more detailed but my memory of the diagram is as shown.

[cxxxi] I Do not Have Enough Faith to be an Atheist, by Dr. Norm Geisler and Frank Turek. Pg 290-293

[cxxxii] I Do not Have Enough Faith to be an Atheist, by Dr. Norm Geisler and Frank Turek. Pg 279

[cxxxiii] Romans 10:14

[cxxxiv] http://www.reasonablefaith.org/st-augustine-said-what

[cxxxv] Steven Weinberg. Dreams of a Final Theory: The Scientist's Search for the Ultimate Laws of Nature. Knopf Doubleday Publishing Group. ISBN 978-0-307-78786-6.

[cxxxvi] 1 Corinthians 23

[cxxxvii] Romans 3:23-24

[cxxxviii] Reasonable Faith, Christian Truth and Apologetics, 3rd Edition, by William Lane Craig, Crossway 2008, Pg 55

[cxxxix] Pew Research Center, America's Changing Religious Landscape, May 12, 2015 and independent analysis by Brace E. Barber

CPSIA information can be obtained
at www.ICGtesting.com
ned in the USA
158181222
2B/369